Journey

on the Level

Owen Shieh

Bro. Bob,

Safe tracks,

Owen Shieh

ISBN 978-0-615-45288-3

First edition: April 2011
Second edition: May 2011

Cover photos by Nicholas Engerer.

The author welcomes any comments and feedback. He can
be reached at **Owen@JourneyOnTheLevel.com**.

To continue the journey with fellow travelers via an online
discussion forum or to order more copies of this book,
please visit **www.JourneyOnTheLevel.com**.

To my longtime friend,
Brother Daniel Herr,
for without his inspiration,
I would not have knocked
on the western door.

Contents

Author's Note

The journey of life, the greatest mystery of all the mysteries known to man, has been the ongoing saga of our species from time immemorial. Through the countless pages of history, we have transitioned from caves to suburbs, from spears to fighter jets, and from hieroglyphs to literary masterpieces. Yet we are still searching for the solution of this great mystery as our travels aboard this terrestrial spaceship continue without pause. For generations, we have sought to answer the deepest questions of our existence; thousands of belief systems and religions have flourished and waned; and the bloodiest wars have been fought over our attempts to confront the essence of our humanity. Alas, the great paradox lies with our inability to understand the very thing that we are, like an artist inside his living room who fails to see the color of the exterior of his own home.

In our travels as a human species, institutions have been developed to embrace our collective humanity, regardless of religion, culture, or social status. Some have promoted the ideals of democracy, carried the torch of freedom, and provided a voice for the most creative minds. Some have encouraged all the actors in this great journey of life to come together and unite in the face of uncertainty, to respect each other no matter the creed, and to reach across boundaries – both natural and manmade – that cannot touch our collective human spirit.

Through the damage of ignorance, the scourge of war, and the crash of empires, a select few of these noble institutions have survived because of their adherence to the fundamental, universal principles of man. *Journey on the Level* is a book about our personal journey of life, framed within the context of the symbolism associated with one such institution – Freemasonry.

It has been said that approximately 100,000 books have been written about Freemasonry. The only individual topics to have surpassed this number are national histories and religious texts. So why add another Masonic book to the list? While many of these published works have beautifully interpreted the compelling histories, noble tenets, and deepest philosophies of Freemasonry, few have focused attention squarely on the application of them to our daily lives outside the lodge room. *Journey on the Level* fills that void.

As Entered Apprentices, we are admonished to build "that house not made with hands," but exactly what does this entail? Ultimately, only each individual brother can truly answer this question for himself. Yet there is much we can do to more deeply understand how to incorporate the symbols of Freemasonry into our daily lives, outside of the lodge room, outside of the ritual. The art of seeing and living by the ideals of Freemasonry brings indescribable rewards to any brother who seeks them. If we were to accomplish the lofty goal of challenging ourselves to see the world in a different light, with the guidance of the "Three Great Lights of Masonry," then philosophies would no longer be philosophies. They would simply become an integral part of our minds and consciousnesses.

Since there are many readers who find the esoteric language of the old classics of Masonic literature a bit out of reach, this book presents Masonic symbolism and philosophy in a contemporary context, complete with language and analogies from the 21st century. It is my hope that this book will reach a diverse audience across the worldwide Masonic fraternity, appealing to brothers of all faiths, cultures, and philosophical interests. Our mutual search for Truth and spiritual enlightenment, regardless of background or context, strikes a chord at the heart of man.

It was with these ideas in mind that I began this book project. I am indebted to my Masonic mentor, Brother Travis Roberts of Norman Lodge No. 38 in Oklahoma, for showing me the importance of fostering fraternal trust and personal inspiration through proper mentoring. Through the years, I have striven to follow in his footsteps by volunteering to serve as an official or unofficial "mentor" to Masonic candidates going through their degrees in Oklahoma, Colorado, and Hawai'i. But I soon found out that the very acts of teaching proficiencies, expressing my ideas, and listening to the brothers' interpretations resulted in fresh insights and original realizations that I would not have otherwise acquired. Thus, instead of the term "mentoring," I prefer to call such Masonic discussions "conversations."

Whether it was guiding brothers through their proficiencies or joining them on philosophical tangents late into the night, I learned more about their life stories, about my own place in the world, and about the true value of Freemasonry during those conversations than I ever have in the tyled lodge room! During one memorable experience, I backpacked into the alpine Rocky Mountain wilderness and taught parts of the Master Mason proficiency while gazing at a panoramic cliff face carved with multiple waterfalls on the edge of an expansive, glacial valley. Surely, Freemasonry is much more than just history and tradition. The greatest reward of being a Mason is to look into the eyes of a fellow brother and *know* that there exists a mutual trust and understanding that cannot be expressed with words. We all have friends at work, friends at school, friends who play sports with us, and friends with whom we hang out on the weekends. But to have friends who explore the essence of life with us and commit to such an adventure – indeed, they are rare gifts.

Journey on the Level is a product of countless hours of Masonic conversations with my fellow brothers, young and old. Since my own initiation, I have often kept a little pocket notebook with me to jot down those rare moments of insight that arise spontaneously. By nurturing these, with relatively little effort, I have found that they have changed my life for the better. In effect, every friend and fellow Mason I have ever crossed paths with has contributed indirectly to this book. Ideas in the following pages can often be traced back to a moment of realization I had during a particular conversation or during a moment of solitary reflection. If each reader, regardless of his personal level of interest or enthusiasm for Masonic philosophy, can find just a single idea meaningful in this book, then the goal of this work would be accomplished.

This book is organized as follows: the first three chapters describe the journey of an Entered Apprentice; the fourth chapter follows the practice of a Fellow Craft; and the last three chapters delve into the core of the wisdom of the Master Mason by pointing to the deepest philosophies of impermanence and introspection. With respect to the reader's journey: the first three chapters take him outside the norm of his habitual thoughts; the first five chapters together elevate him to a higher level of critical analysis of his daily life; and all seven chapters as a whole direct him to continue down his path of life as a true and faithful Master Mason.

The symbolisms of the three degrees are intricately contained within the beautiful and often poetic language of Masonic ritual. While philosophy and interpretation can be freely discussed, the elements of ritual that cannot be written down are not included in this book. Special care has been taken not to reveal the specific names or words of particular symbols that are non-monitorial, but the experienced Mason should be able to read between the lines. Furthermore, among the monitorial symbols, only those that were deemed acceptable for all readers, regardless of degree, were included. Since this issue may be subject to different opinions depending on jurisdiction, the works of other highly respected Masonic authors were used as a general guideline to determine which topics would be appropriate to include and which to exclude.

If this book will be used as guided reading for candidates awaiting initiation or for brothers in the process of preparing their degree proficiencies, his mentor is welcome to decide which chapters would be appropriate to assign. It may be prudent in some situations to allow the brother to experience his degrees with absolutely no preconceptions, so as to ensure the originality of his own experience. However, this book in its entirety may be a good resource for the philosophically-minded candidate or brother to start the practice of introspection even before completing all three degrees, so that he can approach his experiences with the proper mindset. I leave it to the reader to decide.

A unique aspect of Freemasonry is its non-dogmatic and non-sectarian approach to encouraging its members to ponder life's greatest questions and to think for themselves. The ideas presented in this book are spiritual and philosophical in nature but do not pertain to any particular religion. Although Freemasonry itself is *not* a religion, it has been said that all the elements and events within a Masonic lodge can be associated with analogy to the mental realm. Even though it uses Biblical allegory, Freemasonry is a unique institution because it preserves an aspect of introspection and contemplation that has been lost in many of the mainstream, modern-day, Western belief systems. This book will challenge us to view symbols in ways we may not have encountered before.

Journey on the Level is meant to be reflective and thought provoking, so it should be read slower than a typical novel. While reading, please keep in mind that nobody has the right or authority to speak on behalf of the entirety of Freemasonry, nor can he profess knowledge of a strict interpretation of a particular symbol. All the ideas presented in this book are my own insights and opinions only – not to be taken as universal interpretations. The reader should not be afraid to pause and critically analyze how each concept can be applied to daily life before proceeding. If, upon trial and experimentation using sound logic and reason, he finds a particular idea to be incompatible with his experiences, then there is certainly no obligation to adopt it. However, I wholeheartedly encourage the reader to approach all of the concepts in this book with a receptive mind, so that he may reap the fullest rewards. But this book is not meant to provide all the answers. Instead, the reader should use it as a launching point to find his own.

For the general audience, may this work provide some useful, philosophical insight and shed light on the practical meanings behind some of the symbols that have been passed down through innumerable generations of Freemasons. Even though there are specific membership requirements and privileges within Freemasonry, the philosophy of "Brotherly Love, Relief, and Truth" is to be shared with the world. After all, life is but a journey, regardless of names, titles, or membership dues.

For the scholar or historian seeking to evaluate the nature of Freemasonry under the occasional cloak of public misperception, see it as a source of inspiration for many, rather than the object of misconstrued cynicism for a few. Freemasonry is not perfect. No institutions of man are ever perfect, even those with the greatest and noblest of ideals toward which to strive. So judge not the integrity of an institution based on the actions of a few. Instead, understand that any institution that encourages reflection and develops compassion among its constituents *as a whole* is one that is noble and worthy of acclaim. Freemasonry is a means to an end of self-improvement, not the end. It is a constant work in progress. May this book serve as a testament to that work.

For the new initiate as well as the seasoned Master Mason, I hope that this book will serve as a reliable and trusty companion along your journey. When "life gets in the way," it is easy to place activities such as Freemasonry on the backburner, but it is in those lessons inculcated in your Masonic experience where you will find the answers that will help you deal with life's challenges. Diligent study of the monitor, which is given to all Master Masons (depending on jurisdiction), together with the guidance contained within the pages of this book, will serve as a good starting point from which you can begin to reap the benefits of a colorful and personally rewarding Masonic experience that extends well beyond the tyled door.

May the words contained within these pages serve as a spark that ignites a flame of inspiration within your breast to continue on your inward journey and seek your own answers to life's most pressing questions. The last section of this book, "Reflections," is for you to jot down your own thoughts and realizations as you read, so that you can complete the story of your journey in your own way. When you stop to take a sip of water or to rest on a rock next to a babbling brook, use those last few pages to record your own thoughts and to document your own strokes of insight. Someday, when you look back at your notes, you may realize that they have changed the course of your life for the better.

Come. Let us embark upon this journey with these words from Brother Mark Twain in mind:

Twenty years from now you will be more disappointed by the things that you didn't do than by the ones you did do. So throw off the bowlines. Sail away from the safe harbor. Catch the trade winds in your sails. Explore. Dream. Discover.

Bon voyage!

OWEN H. SHIEH

EDUCATION COMMITTEE COACH
HONOLULU LODGE
GRAND LODGE OF HAWAI'I F. & A.M.

CERTIFICATE LECTURER (2010, CLASS "C")
NORMAN LODGE NO. 38
GRAND LODGE OF OKLAHOMA A.F. & A.M.

HONOLULU
APRIL 2011

Foreword

I am frequently asked, "What is Freemasonry?" It is an organization that is often shrouded in mystery and misunderstood by not only the uninitiated, but also its own members. So when Brother Owen Shieh asked me to review *Journey on the Level*, I was excited to see another Mason's point of view about the Craft. Since meeting Brother Shieh, I have found him to be a serious lover of Masonry, thoughtful about its ideals and principles, and hungry to discover its endless layers of complexity. I am very honored to have been asked to write this foreword.

Journey on the Level offers a fresh perspective on the philosophical aspects of the three degrees as seen through the eyes of a young man in his search for the meaning of Freemasonry. Brother Shieh takes the reader from the darkness of ignorance, in which we all find ourselves at some point in our lives, to the light of understanding. He challenges us to look at the various hurdles that life throws our way and to apply the principles of Freemasonry to overcome them.

Written in the tone of a friendly dialogue, the author invites the reader to join him on an adventure. He leads a sojourn through the depths of symbolism that form the core of Masonic philosophy. During the journey, the reader is encouraged to question, to observe, and to contemplate. Rather than professing the universality of a single perspective, this book inspires the reader to develop original thoughts and ideas beyond the words contained.

Journey on the Level is easy to understand and is laced with poignant quotes from great thinkers throughout history. These are supplemented with wonderful, personal anecdotes from the author's own experiences. Particularly notable is his section about "the train," an especially thought-provoking analysis of the value of recognizing one's emotions and their effects. Many of the ideas in the book could serve as excellent topics to inspire discussion in Masonic education segments either during or after lodge meetings. Through the frequent use of analogies that connect symbols to the everyday world, the author guides and encourages the reader to apply Masonic wisdom to the improvement of daily life outside of the lodge.

Journey on the Level successfully melds four major approaches to Masonic philosophy. It combines the intellectual philosophies of Preston's system of knowledge and Krause's system of morals with those of Oliver's system of traditions and Pike's system of symbolism – all done in a way the common man can understand. For longtime members of Freemasonry, this book will inspire creative ways of approaching and interpreting familiar, Masonic symbols. For those who have been newly introduced to the fraternity, this will serve as a solid foundation to start your own lifelong adventure. For our friends and families who have wondered with curiosity about the essence of the Craft, this book will be enjoyable and enlightening. For all, this work concisely captures the spirit of the practical science and noble art of Freemasonry.

I highly recommend *Journey on the Level* to anyone who seeks to understand Freemasonry and its effects on the individuals who choose to walk its paths. This is a book that is sure to be a great addition to any Masonic library. May your own journey be filled with wonder and excitement.

MONTY J. GLOVER

GRAND MASTER
GRAND LODGE OF HAWAI'I F. & A.M.

HONOLULU
APRIL 2011

Acknowledgments

First and foremost, I am indebted to my family for supporting me in all of my endeavors since my youthful years in Florida and beyond: to my mother, Lily, for her unspeakable love and personal guidance since well before I uttered my first word; to my father, Charles, for his untiring and selfless support of my academic and professional development; and to my brother, Jason, for growing up with me and sharing those memorable moments of life and scenes from childhood that only true brothers can understand. May this book and its merits serve as a testament to the immense contribution of my family to who I am today. I owe my life to them in more ways than I can count.

I must thank Brother Daniel Herr, my friend and fellow traveler from my undergraduate years at Cornell University, who encouraged my philosophical development well before we encountered Freemasonry. Over the years, he has helped me realize that a genuine friendship is a rare gem to be treasured, regardless of where we reside. This book is dedicated to him, for being the first to inspire me to see life as nothing but a journey with a wide expanse of possibilities and challenges.

My Masonic journey would not have been possible without the guidance and devotion of Brother Travis Roberts, my mentor from Norman Lodge No. 38 in Norman, Oklahoma. As a fledgling Mason, I spent countless hours in discussion with him in his office at home, orally learning the full proficiencies of all three degrees line-by-line – a process that took months to master, but with sublime rewards that will last a lifetime. His level of devotion to Freemasonry is unsurpassed, and I constantly strive to follow in his footsteps. Many thanks go to Brother Daniel Hanttula, who was the first to suggest that I someday write a book about Masonic philosophy; to Brother Clayton Daily for being my first mentee and whose friendship exemplified the irreplaceable camaraderie that can come from teaching and learning degree proficiencies; to Brothers Ray Stone, George Lanzidelle, Gary Bailey, Louis Khoury, Jeremy Orosco, Josh King, Clayton Hoskinson, and all the other brothers of Norman Lodge No. 38 for contributing to the beginning of my journey. No matter where the trail of life may take me, Norman will always be my Masonic home.

Other Masons from Oklahoma have contributed significantly to my personal growth: Therin Miller, for encouraging me to write this book, for his inspirational life of honor and integrity to his family and country, and for being a genuine and faithful friend who makes my Masonic journey completely worth the time and effort; Colt Looper, for his innate ability to see and apply the lessons of Freemasonry to his life, no matter the difficulties; and Josh Overvig, for never ceasing to question and to think outside the box. Our many late-night conversations about the interpretations of Masonic degrees were enlightening.

During my brief stay in Colorado in the summer of 2010, I met several Masons with whom conversations led to some of the concepts presented in this book. Thus, they deserve my utmost gratitude. Thanks go to Brother Stefan Moran, for living a life of service and whose devotion to self-improvement inspires me to be a better person each day; and to Brother Brian Murphy, for exhibiting the strength of resolve and an unshakeable faith for doing what is right, no matter how high the hurdle – a virtue that I aspire to achieve. The mutual trust that developed from the many Masonic conversations we shared proved that within the Masonic fraternity, good friends might only be just around the corner. To see such great examples of young Masons who strive to uphold the values of the fraternity gives me the faith to strive on. Thanks to their encouragement, this book is now a reality.

I am grateful for Brother Ryan Klassy, who was the first Mason to welcome me to Colorado. His friendliness, positive attitude, and tireless devotion to the new generation of Masons never cease to inspire. Thanks also go to Brothers Charlie Plagainos and Bruce Yelen, who accompanied me to memorable Masonic events. My experiences in Colorado contributed greatly to my journey, so I must recognize the following lodges for hosting my visits: Boulder Lodge No. 45, Columbia Lodge No. 14, Nevada Lodge No. 4, Denver Lodge No. 5, Centennial Lodge No. 84, Estes Park Lodge No. 183, Fidelity Lodge No. 192, and Northglenn Lodge No. 194. Special thanks go to Centennial Lodge No. 84, for voting me as an honorary member of their lodge. I am sincerely humbled.

The final version of this book would not have been possible without the following brothers in Hawai'i who reviewed the drafts and offered helpful feedback: Michael Wright, Stephan Fabel, Monty Glover, Justin McNeal, RJ Kapuscinski, and Greg Pentecost. Thanks also go to Les Fukushima for her comments about the initial manuscript. To all the brothers of Honolulu Lodge and Schofield Lodge, thank you for making me feel at home since the first day of my arrival on these beautiful Hawai'ian Islands.

Special thanks go to Brother Greg Pentecost, for his unwavering devotion to the cause of Masonic education in Hawai'i. His Masonic Education Dinners, held three times a year, present a forum for constructive discussion about all elements of Masonic philosophy, history, and tradition. With brothers throughout Hawai'i contributing as speakers, these events enhance the traditional spirit of Masonic dialogue. The theme of this book was solidified during the first of these dinners. I strongly encourage all Master Masons visiting or residing in Hawai'i to participate!

The abovementioned brothers include students, businessmen, nurses, paramedics, Marines, soldiers, veterans, pastors, scientists, engineers, teachers, and other professionals – people from all walks of life, contributing to an organization that has thrived for centuries. Many of those acknowledged here are only in their twenties. No doubt, the future of Freemasonry rests in good hands.

Several of my friends unaffiliated with Freemasonry have contributed greatly to my life journey and to the ideas contained within this book, and they deserve my utmost respect and gratitude. There was no person more intimately tied to my spiritual and philosophical development during my time in Oklahoma than my good friend Nicholas Engerer. Our backpacking trips and adventures vastly expanded my physical and mental horizons. From deserts to alpine lakes, from prairies to snow-capped mountains, from tornadoes to monasteries – we left no stones unturned, no thoughts unscrutinized, and no possibilities unexplored. Regardless of the separate journeys that we must now take, his contribution to my life adventure will always be preserved in his photographs that comprise the covers of this book.

Thanks go to Kevin Ballantine, whose unfailing strength and positive attitude against the toughest odds inspire all who know him. His fortitude and humor have been a true inspiration for me since my years in college. Thanks also go to Stephen Mullens, for showing me the importance of constructive, religious dialogue and the beauty of the strength of a friendship grounded not on what we believe, but on our mutual care for Truth, humanity, and the pursuit of science. Finally, I must acknowledge Ven. Jian Hu and Ven. Jian Mao for their guidance over the years and for instilling within my heart the motivation for self-improvement and the pursuit of my spiritual quest to seek life's deepest mysteries.

Journey on the Level

Introduction to Freemasonry

The ancient and honorable craft of Freemasonry has had a long and storied past. At once a community service organization as well as a deeply philosophical and historical entity, Freemasonry in the modern world is a fraternity that exists in a category of its own. Throughout history, it has shaped the evolution of civilization by offering a platform for freethinkers and men to help each other become better citizens and better people. How did Freemasonry distill into its current form through the ages? A common and almost trite phrase that has been used to summarize the essence of the Craft states, "Freemasonry is a system of morality, veiled in allegory, and illustrated by symbols." But why symbols? And why bother with allegory? To answer these questions, we must briefly discuss the history of Freemasonry.

The exact beginnings of the teachings and philosophy of Freemasonry are lost in time. Many of the symbols and ideas that were adopted into the ritual were no doubt related to the philosophical ideas prevalent throughout the Old World. Some have suggested that the ancient philosophies of China, Egypt, Rome, and other civilizations have contributed to the development of Masonic symbolism. Although much of the allegory and symbolism of Masonic ritual come from Abrahamic religious traditions, it is clear that much of the philosophy can be traced deep into history prior to the development of organized Western religion.

The term "Freemason" is known to have existed as early as the year 1212, and the Regius Poem of 1390 is one of the oldest known Masonic documents. It discussed the topic of geometry and the importance of moral guidelines alongside the operation of construction projects. During the Middle Ages, when the building of cathedrals was a prominent trade throughout Europe, guilds of stonemasons were widespread. The operative Freemasons were part of the select few who had the privilege of traveling freely between cities to obtain work. As such, they guarded their cathedral-building craft intensely and trained the juniors in their trade through a master-apprentice system.

Unlike their specialized, modern-day counterparts, the cathedral builders of the Middle Ages were not just construction workers; they were scholars, philosophers, artists, writers, mathematicians, and community leaders. During that time, since formal education was primarily restricted to the domain of the Church, the highly educated Freemasons appealed to many. Those who wished to join in the fellowship, particularly scholars, were eventually accepted into the group and became speculative Freemasons. As such, the fraternity in its modern form was born.

Freedom of thought, expression of intellect, and promotion of liberty formed the mutual interests of the early Freemasons during the Age of Enlightenment. Within these lodges of members, they found solace in their mutual bond that was founded upon not only their trade, but also their philosophical interests. In the age of monarchies and religious intolerance, this was a comfortable abode for those whose thirst for mental freedom yearned to break free. After the Reformation and the age of the great cathedrals began to decline, Freemasonry evolved and became speculative, dominated mostly by accepted members rather than those who were trained in cathedral building.

In London, on 24 June 1717, the first organization of several Masonic lodges appeared, and the Grand Lodge of England was born. However, due to differences in opinion over the standardization of Masonic philosophy and ritual, a solid foundation upon which a global Masonic fraternity could rest did not materialize until the formation of the United Grand Lodge of England on 25 November 1813. Since then, the grand lodge system has served as a standard by which "regular" or "mainstream" Masonic lodges are organized.

Masonic lodges spread quickly throughout Europe, Asia, and the Americas, and today, lodges exist worldwide. With around six million members, Freemasonry has been described as the oldest and largest fraternity in existence. However, despite popular myths, it does not have a governing body on the global scale. In fact, any semblance of organization and standardization of ritual between grand lodge jurisdictions relies solely upon the adherence to fixed traditions, or "landmarks," and mouth-to-ear instruction between master and apprentice that has existed since "time immemorial." In the United States, where approximately 1.5 million men are Freemasons, each state operates under a separate and sovereign grand lodge. While they can trace their roots back to the United Grand Lodge of England, they do not have any national governing body that oversees their activities.

Today, the techniques and tools used by the early, operative Freemasons are taken as symbols for constructing our mental and spiritual edifices, rather than actual buildings made of stone. Any honest, upright man of good reputation and character may apply for membership in any Masonic lodge, pending an investigation and interview by a committee and a favorable, unanimous vote by lodge members. Members cannot recruit a man to join. Prospective members must *ask* to join. This is to ascertain that all candidates are approaching this fraternity of their own choice and free will. The greatest achievements and accomplishments in human history have come from the will and volition that originates from a person's heart and mind, divorced from any form of coercion. Thus it is with Freemasonry. A person who is willing to take upon himself a journey of personal and philosophical discovery must do so on his own accord.

A few other prerequisites for membership in a Masonic lodge are worth noting. Depending upon the grand lodge jurisdiction, a man must be at least a certain age. In some jurisdictions the minimum age is 18, whereas in others the minimum age may be 21. This is for the obvious reason of making sure that the candidate is fit to think on his own. Mental and intellectual independence is of utmost importance in Freemasonry, given the reasons already described.

The candidate must also believe in a "supreme being." Some jurisdictions may refer to this as "God" or, in order to maintain religious neutrality, the "Grand Architect of the Universe." The important thing to note is that even though much of the ritual is based upon Biblical allegory, the institution of Freemasonry is absolutely committed to religious freedom and dialogue. In fact, it encourages its members to hold steadfast and diligently practice the religion of their choosing, rather than imposing one belief over another. The idea and conceptualization of a "supreme being" can be highly dependent upon the religious ideas of the candidate. Regardless of the names assigned to "Truth," the key point is that the candidate must believe that there is something more, something unknown, and something beyond our limited understanding of the material world – something that relates to the underlying order of the universe and to the true nature of our consciousnesses. Howsoever the candidate would like to define "supreme being" is entirely up to him.

Upon acceptance, the candidate is led through three degrees, or ceremonies, that use ritual, lecture, and symbolism to convey the deepest philosophies that have been passed down through Freemasons for countless generations. The degrees are serious, solemn events that encourage the candidate to think and reflect upon important questions in life. The first degree is the Entered Apprentice. Upon its completion, depending on the jurisdiction, the newly initiated brother is assigned to a mentor who teaches and guides him through some memory work. This is designed to solidify the details of the ritual in the mind of the brother. He then must pass a "proficiency," or oral recitation of what he memorized in front of his lodge, before he can move on to his second degree: the Fellow Craft. The same process continues until he qualifies for his third and final degree, the Master Mason. He then officially assumes full membership in the fraternity.

The three degrees reflect the method of instruction that was employed by the operative Freemasons of the Middle Ages. During the process, the brother learns the history, philosophy, and traditions of the fraternity; but more importantly, he is challenged to think creatively and independently about his intellectual and spiritual place in society. He also takes a set of obligations, whereby he vows to commit himself to the journey of self-improvement and to help those around him do the same.

So why symbols? And why allegory? Why are they necessary during the conferral of degrees? Unlike the traditional forms of learning that occur in schools, where lessons are taught explicitly as lectures in the classroom, Freemasonry teaches through the communication of symbols. While this may seem like an indirect method of teaching, it forces the brother to find his own answers to the questions posed; it challenges him to see that the *act* of finding answers, *in itself*, is a journey that is valuable. In the end, the man who discovers the answers and experiences them directly is the one who will permanently treat them as his most prized possessions. As such, the power of understanding Truth through symbol and allegory cannot be understated. For example, we can instruct each individual driver of all the cars on the road to hit the brakes at a particular time at each intersection. Or, we can teach the *symbolism* of the color red and the white letters "STOP" placed within an octagon, and leave it up to each individual driver to understand the implied instruction no matter where or when a stop sign is encountered. Which method is more efficient? Once the driver knows that a symbol implies "stop the vehicle," he can then apply it to each particular circumstance, taking into consideration road conditions, traffic density, and speed of the vehicle, without being explicitly instructed each time. To specify an instruction for each individual occasion would be impossible, given the infinite combinations of circumstances. Thus, understanding a symbol is much more powerful than receiving a series of explicit instructions.

Finally, it would be prudent to address the issue of why only men are allowed to join Freemasonry. Such a requirement may seem archaic at first, given the accepted equality between men and women in modern society. Freemasonry most certainly acknowledges the fundamental equality of all human beings, regardless of gender, race, religion, or social status. The primary reason for its male-only membership rests purely on its status as a *fraternity*. Like any other fraternal organization, membership is typically divided among gender lines. This fosters a sense of "brotherhood" or "sisterhood" among its members that enhances trust and camaraderie between those who may share particular challenges and philosophies in life. Many organizations directly affiliated with Freemasonry, in fact, allow the membership of women, some of which are women-only sororities. Beyond the realm of fraternities and sororities, many other organizations, such as the Boy Scouts and Girl Scouts, are divided among gender lines. This is not to denigrate the equality of men and women, but rather, to promote a special type of bond and mutual support among the members of each gender.

Given the increased visibility of Freemasonry in recent media and popular culture, many lodges are experiencing a new surge in young membership. This bodes well for the continuation of an organization that has made "good men better" for generations. But unfortunately, throughout history, there have been some misunderstandings about the fraternity that have been perpetuated by conspiracy theorists, totalitarian forms of government, and those who are *not* proponents of religious freedom. For example, the ludicrous speculation that Freemasons are plotting world domination can easily be shattered by the simple fact that there is no global organization that governs the role of the grand lodges. The list of famous Freemasons is not an indication of an attempt at global control. Rather, the large proportion of prestigious Masonic alumni is likely due to the fact that the reasons for a person's success are intimately tied to the same reasons that he would have an appeal for Freemasonry – the presence of an inner desire for self-improvement and the improvement of society at large. In short, correlation is not causation. These and other myths have been discussed at length by other authors, and the reader is directed to two contemporary and easily-accessible books that elaborate on this topic: *The Complete Idiot's Guide to Freemasonry* by S. Brent Morris and *Freemasons for Dummies* by Christopher Hodapp.

False rumors have been perpetuated throughout history by totalitarian regimes that suppress grassroots organizations or institutions that promote freedom of speech, freedom of religion, and the ideals of democracy. These are principles that Freemasonry holds near and dear. It has been said that the governing principles of the United States are a "Masonic experiment." No doubt, many of our founding fathers such as Brothers George Washington, John Hancock, and Benjamin Franklin had Masonic principles in mind when they began the arduous task of drafting the Constitution of a new nation founded on the principles of "life, liberty, and the pursuit of happiness."

Freemasonry has also come under attack by some conservative religious movements, where the ideals of religious freedom and independent thought are called into question. To those critics, an organization meeting "on the level" with respect to members following different religions could be deemed sacrilegious or even blasphemous with respect to their own particular religious beliefs. Yet it is the coexistence of freedom of thought and mutual respect that is truly one of humanity's greatest capabilities and one of the noble tenets of Freemasonry.

While philosophical in nature, Freemasonry is not a religion. In fact, sectarian religion and partisan politics are not to be discussed in lodge, because these are topics that could be most damaging to a brotherhood, as the history of the world has taught us. Philosophy and world affairs can and should be discussed, as all Masons should hold those topics in high esteem. However, claiming the dominance of one particular viewpoint over another is forbidden. The term "ritual" is simply used to describe traditional activities that are solemn and orderly, not as a reference to anything religious or sectarian. Rather, Freemasonry uses symbols – irrespective of faith – to encourage us to think more deeply about life, and in effect, brings like-minded men together in pursuit of a solid, unshakeable brotherhood of compassion and trust. Rarely do we see a richly philosophical organization foster such close bonds between men of widely different religious faiths, each devoted to each other's welfare and to the improvement of himself as a human being and son of Mother Earth.

I

From Darkness to Light

Imagine a group of men sitting on chairs inside a cave, facing the interior wall. These men have lived in this cave their entire lives, never once stepping foot outside. They were born and raised here. Furthermore, they have always sat in these chairs, not able to move any limbs or even turn their heads, because they are physically chained to the chairs. Behind them lies the opening of the cave, where there exists a blazing fire. In front of the fire on the side facing the cave, people walk by with various figures made of stone and wood. Shadows of these figures are cast against the interior wall of the cave, which the men see with their eyes. The noises from outside the cave echo from the wall and reach their ears as reflections of sound. With their limited senses and perspectives, they speak to each other and describe the shadows they see before them. They take those shadows to be true representations of reality. They name them. They study them. They grow fond of some, while rejecting others. They debate and argue over the essence of the shadows. Some even get angry over their disagreements about what the shadows represent. After much study, a select few of the men begin to understand and predict the behavior of the shadows and sounds. Since there is no knowledge of anything beyond, their counterparts praise them for their superior intellect and ability to understand the world.

Now imagine that one of the men is released from his restraints and forced to exit the cave. At first he protests, not willing to let go of the images on the wall, because those shadows were his life and reality, as he knew it. But after some time outside the cave, he begins to understand and appreciate the abundance of colors, the warmth of the sun, and the glory of realizing the essence of life beyond what society had once dictated to him. He learns to question. He learns to think critically. He learns to *experience* the truth of life, rather than simply relying on conjecture and blind faith. He understands the importance of practice and "walking the walk." He realizes the foolishness of the men in the cave who spend time arguing, bickering, hating, judging, and competing over their own interpretations of the shadows, not knowing that they are simply shadows and that their interpretations are flawed. He loses his fear of confronting and questioning that which his counterparts have deemed "just how life is supposed to be."

Suppose this man returns to the cave. He greets the men who are still chained to their respective chairs and attempts to communicate what he had just experienced outside the cave. He tries his best to explain the colors, the sights, the sounds, the smells, and the feelings; but alas, he finds no words in the language of his fellow men that can adequately describe what he had just *experienced.* So he resorts to the use of allegory and symbolism. But he finds that most of them cannot seem to see past the symbols. They either take them too literally or do not care for them at all. As his last resort, he encourages the men to join him on the journey out of the cave. They protest, as he once did. They question his motives. Their emotions and habits for judgment become habitually directed toward him, and he is deemed to be either naïve or an out-of-touch idealist. Worse, they accuse him of trying to impose his own crazy ideas upon the rest of them. He feels sorry for the men, but realizes out of compassion that he was once in their shoes.

The original version of this story was told millennia ago by the Greek philosopher Plato. His famous "Allegory of the Cave," found in his work, *The Republic*, hauntingly describes the state of humanity. We are the men in the cave. We are the men who are chained to the chairs. We are the men who spend our entire lives seeing an illusion – a reflection of reality. This illusion is naturally brought about by our limited senses and perspectives, and yet, our egos chain us to the chairs. We always think we're right. It's us versus them. It's me versus you. If you're not with me, then you're against me. And so, the most frightening part is – we do not even recognize our situation! Rarely do we question societal norms. Rarely do we try to step outside the box and see things from a different perspective. Rarely do we see our own mistakes. Rarely do we acknowledge our faults. Rarely do we learn from them.

We spend our lives categorizing things, conceptualizing them, and then passing judgment based on our own biases and limited perspectives. Without even taking a brief moment to think from another's perspective, we readily misunderstand the full picture – the reality of a given situation. We disagree with our friends. We argue with our wives. We get angry at circumstances that do not follow our desires. We get frustrated at events we cannot control. In short, we *misunderstand* each other and ourselves...all the time. And not once do we step back and wonder, "What am I doing??" We are victims of *ignorance*. To deny this would be a further sign of ignorance.

Ignorance is the perpetual human condition. Symbolized by darkness, ignorance is our habitual lack of understanding, empathy, and foresight. It is our state of not seeing the full picture. It is not being fully aware of the reality of life and the events contained therein. It is being inside a box – or a cave – without even knowing that we are in one! Furthermore, we are trapped by our egos. We think that what we perceive is unequivocally true, neglecting the fact that our perspectives are often limited. When we see the shadows on the wall, it is not that we refuse to question their true nature, but rather, we do not even recognize that they are shadows in the first place! We think they are real. We think that is all there is. We think how we feel about someone or something is *real* and *absolute*. But our feelings about people or things are nothing but our own mental images – shadows of reality – not reality itself. What we *think* may often not be how it *is*. Our thoughts are mental projections. Like a picture on the wall created by an overhead projector in a classroom, our mental thoughts are only partial reflections of reality. What we think is undeniable fact may often be only opinion. By confusing the projection of someone for the reality of that person, we give rise to interpersonal misunderstandings. I think you're this-and-that. You think I'm such-and-such. And we both disagree about our personal assessments of each other. The result? Conflict.

We seek to satisfy our inner hunger for light, for understanding, for wisdom, for happiness. But, like a hungry person who does not realize that he needs proper nourishment and instead attempts to temporarily satisfy his hunger with junk food, we seek money, power, fame, and sensory pleasures – all of which may bring about negative consequences, again because of our lack of foresight. And so, we are trapped in a violent rollercoaster of dualistic emotions – likes, dislikes, love, hatred, selfishness, envy, licentiousness – unceasing turbulence of the mind that leads to vexations. This is not to say that a particular emotion is inherently "good" or inherently "bad." Nothing is *inherently* anything. Rather, it is our confusion of what we really need for what we *think* we need that causes the vexations. Like those first rays of sun that shine through the dark clouds after a torrential thunderstorm, wisdom and understanding together serve as beacons of peace and sanity, chasing away the shadows of our ignorance. With wisdom comes true and lasting happiness.

This is where we begin. This is where we begin our journey from darkness to light. To acknowledge our state of ignorance is to take the first step of this journey. A person who is obese must first recognize his problem before he can begin a new diet and exercise regimen. A miserly millionaire must first realize that money cannot enrich his heart before he can become willing to donate to charity. A person who seeks to quit smoking must first acknowledge the long-term health consequences of continuing. Without this *self-realization*, nothing can be done to convince a person to change himself for the better. The change must first come from *within*. Otherwise, he will put forth a level of resistance much like the men in the cave when asked to step outside. We cannot impose our beliefs on anyone, even if we think the beliefs are correct, even if we think we are trying to help by carrying the torch of virtue. Realization and inspiration cannot be forced. They must arise from within each individual. The most anyone else can do is to help support such inspiration. We each must walk our own journey.

So what is this journey? Where are we going? What is the purpose? The journey that underlies the institution of Freemasonry is one that takes us *inward*. In order to build a better world and a more meaningful life, our first task must be to better understand ourselves. This is the purpose of the working tools of the Entered Apprentice. By "divesting our minds and consciences of all the vices and superfluities of life," we begin to uncover who we truly are – underneath all the emotions, all the vexations, and all the fleeting characteristics that change with time. Like the changing of the weather and the passing of the clouds, we confuse the temporary – our passing thoughts and emotions – for who we really are. It has been said that the Masonic lodge itself represents the psyche of man. All the objects and events that occur in the lodge are symbols for our mental formations. And so our Masonic journey is equivalent to an expedition of introspection. This is one that cannot be taken lightly. As Brother Winston Churchill said:

Courage is what it takes to stand up and speak; courage is also what it takes to sit down and listen.

Our perpetual state of darkness has left us confused. Who are we? Who am I? What am I doing? What is the purpose of my life? Our inability to answer these questions causes a deep, gnawing feeling of emptiness in our minds that leads us to seek temporary solace in the material and the pleasurable, even though these things often do not bring us *lasting* fulfillment. This is not to say that the material and the pleasurable are bad. The shadows in the cave are not bad. The issue at hand is that there is more to life than what we *think*. And that realization is the key to true happiness and fulfillment. Nothing is inherently all good or all bad, as the Masonic symbol of the checkered pavement teaches us. Rather, it is our lack of understanding of the truth that lies behind the illusions that causes our vexations, like the men in the cave who argue and fight over the shadows that they see before them but do not realize the futility of their judgments and passions. So what exactly are these shadows? And what can we do about our situation? To answer these questions, let us begin our journey away from the darkness of ignorance and into the light of wisdom, through the help of Masonic symbolism.

Chapter I

WHAT IS A JOURNEY?

A journey can be defined as an act of traveling from one place to another. This can be a physical event or a mental one. This can be external or internal. Freemasonry is the art of using the physical to express the mental. It is the science of viewing our external environment as a symbol for understanding our inner selves. When combined with the theme of searching for something, for a higher level of wisdom, for "Truth," this journey becomes a pilgrimage or an *expedition*.

An expedition, or a journey toward some goal, is often found in mythology and folklore. Whether it is the search for the Holy Grail, a voyage through the Mediterranean, a descent into the deepest oceanic trench, or climbing the world's tallest mountain, the essence of the expedition is universal. First, the expedition centers on a main character and his travels. Through his trials and travails, he eventually becomes the hero. His expedition usually starts with an abrupt change or transformation. This forces him to leave his comfort zone, to leave the shadows of the cave and the mundane world behind. As the expedition ensues, the hero is beset with many difficult challenges over a long period of time. This tests his mental and physical limits. But after a while, he endures, perseveres, and overcomes those challenges. In that process, he learns about the places he visited and about the people he met along the way. He learns about his own responses to each of the unique challenges. And as a result, *he learns about himself.* Finally, he reaches his destination, but the goal is often a surprise that is unexpected. The treasure chest is not what he had imagined; the end of the rainbow appears different; the summit is not what he had envisioned. Yet the journey was fulfilling. It was rewarding. It was an adventure that cannot be described with words.

All the elements of an expedition are contained within the three degrees of Masonic initiation. In many ways, this is what makes Freemasonry unique among fraternal and civic organizations. Furthermore, the three degrees challenge us to see our lives as journeys. The most rewarding expeditions take a certain length of time, and the three degrees are intended to serve the same purpose. To hastily rush through them without putting much thought into the philosophy contained within the ritual would be to pick an apple from its tree well before it is ripe. Understandably, extenuating circumstances may arise such that a candidate must quickly receive all the degrees of Freemasonry, but when given a choice, it behooves him to choose to take the extra time for these thoughts to sink in. At the very least, the initiate should take time on his own during and after the length of the entire initiation process to think critically about how he can apply the philosophies to his daily life and make them his own. Food that is slow-cooked tastes better for a reason. So it is with Masonic philosophy.

Our journey from darkness to light is a recurring theme in the Masonic degrees. But why is this journey important? Some may say, "oh, philosophy is not for me," or "I'm not one to wax philosophic, so I'll just leave the deep stuff for the people who are really interested." Yet the beauty of Masonic philosophy is that it can be applied to every aspect of our lives, regardless of whether we consider ourselves philosophers or not. It enriches our personal as well as professional lives. I have seen businessmen, pilots, soldiers, students, scientists, lawyers, professors, and police officers benefit from what is taught in lodge – regardless of which faith or religion they follow – as long as they take the time to understand and apply the teachings to their daily lives. We all have a conscious mind, and this is all we need in order to see life in a more rewarding way. When we truly apply Masonic wisdom to our daily lives, we are the ones who reap the benefits.

Dissatisfaction and fear are results of ignorance. Contentment and peace are products of wisdom. If it's dark outside, and you stumble upon a garden hose, someone could easily convince you that the hose is a poisonous snake. Fear of the unknown would then grip you. But, the moment you shine a flashlight on the hose and realize for yourself the true nature of that source of fear and confusion, your unease would immediately dissolve. Even if your flashlight batteries fail and darkness returns, you would remain at ease. Such is the nature of the light of wisdom.

We can all benefit from the journey from darkness to light, from ignorance to wisdom. But our rewards will be directly proportional to our application of these lessons to our daily lives. We must think critically or else our time will be wasted. We get out what we put in. This is true of everything we do in life, not just in Freemasonry. Our biggest hurdle is our tendency to stick to the status quo, to avoid thinking about the reality of the shadows. For many of us, it is natural to follow the easy route, to take the road most traveled, to do nothing to change our age-old habits. The wise Mason chooses to do otherwise.

Ever since elementary and middle school, our peers have often instilled in us the notion that to be nice and to seek self-improvement is "not cool." This peer pressure was then magnified throughout high school. But why has society formed us this way? Is this societal norm even justified? The issues of religion and ethics in the modern world sometimes seem to take a backseat to scientific advancement and technology. They are frequently viewed as archaic or artificial, but are the issues of personal fulfillment and happiness really archaic at all? Or are they as important now as they were 2,000 years ago?

The increase in material pleasures and sensory entertainment in our world today simply do a better job of distracting us from the perennial problems of humanity. They do not permanently satisfy us. When the noise dies down and the excitement wanes, when we take a few minutes to ourselves and sit by a tranquil lake on the outskirts of town, we are left with the same burning questions: Who are we? Why are we here? What's the point of it all? These questions deeply disturb us. For those who attempt to confront them, but do not know how to properly address them, depression can result. For the rest of us, we try to avoid them. In either case, we are not solving the problem. Not knowing any solution, we keep running. We distract ourselves further. We keep ourselves busy to avoid the questions. Or, we cling to blind faith in an effort to comfort ourselves, because it takes work to question and to critically analyze life. But blind faith can be lost when challenges come our way, and then we are once again forced to confront our fears of the unknown. True faith should come from light and wisdom, not blindness and ignorance. Thus, *first-hand experience* and *mental transformation* are absolutely essential if we want to obtain proper insight, which has the ability to lead us to personal fulfillment.

Masonic symbolism can help us realize the underlying essence and value of life. But without putting in the effort to understand and apply the symbols to our daily lives, we remain in the dark, regardless of the degrees and the titles that we may hold in the fraternity. We run like hamsters in wheels, not really knowing why we're running. We just do it. We wake up, eat breakfast, go to work, look forward to lunch, try to work the afternoon without dozing off, come home, watch TV, make dinner, maybe watch more TV, then go to bed. Wash, rinse, and repeat. Now, there is absolutely nothing *wrong* with any of these things, and we all must make a living, but think about how much more rewarding life would be if we could see it as a journey, using every moment to improve ourselves and come closer to answering the perennial questions that plague us!

When we improve ourselves, we reduce our misunderstandings, naturally improve our interactions with those around us, better handle communication between our friends, more wisely deal with those who disagree with us, and by default, become happier and more content – all while making the world a better place. It is a win-win situation for everyone. With this attitude, life becomes rich. Life becomes no less than an adventure. Every day is new and exciting, and even routines become rewarding – all beginning with a different mindset and a change from *within*.

We can say that there is a worthwhile pot of gold at the end of the journey of self-discovery and enlightenment, but this journey is not an all-or-nothing endeavor. Every step counts. Every step brings us to clearer views and more sweeping vistas. Each moment introduces another ray of light into our cave. Each moment brings us closer to true contentment, and life itself becomes valuable and more than just a means to an end.

But enough with the speculation, let's get going. As Brother Rudyard Kipling commanded:

Something hidden. Go and find it. Go and look behind the ranges – something lost behind the ranges. Lost and waiting for you. Go!

So lace up the old hiking boots! I hear a waterfall up ahead. Let's go check it out! I've got my pack on. You ready?

II

The Journey Begins

STEPPING OUTSIDE THE BOX

All expeditions necessarily begin with an abrupt change – an initial transformation. Whether it is leaving home for the first time, entering foreign lands, descending into the unknown depths of the sea, or ascending into harsh alpine conditions, the traveler finds himself in unfamiliar territory. Far from being just a dramatic element of ancient folklore, our lives can be described as a series of journeys. Any "great and important undertaking" that occurs over a period of time typically begins with an experience that is different from the norm, perhaps even initially outside our comfort zones. Leaving home for college, stepping into a military entrance process station, or starting a new business are experiences that are familiar to many of us. These events take us outside the boundaries of our normal, everyday experiences. They challenge us. They open the door to a new way of life. With a distant but often fuzzy goal in mind, we take our first steps into the unknown. We do not know what to expect, and we accept each of the challenges as they come. So begins our Masonic journey.

DIVESTING OUR MINDS

The three degrees of Freemasonry are solemn, sincere ceremonies that use drama and lectures to convey a deeply profound message. This is where tradition and symbolism combine to teach the candidate the arts of the Craft.

The Entered Apprentice degree initiates us into the Masonic fraternity. It places us in the role of the traveler, launching us into our journey with an initial transformation. It challenges us to think beyond the norm. What do we truly own in life? Underneath our material wealth, represented by metallic objects, who are we? What lies beneath our material possessions? The plain and simple garment that was used in the degree was a symbol that called our attention to the fact that our *true nature* is not defined by how we look or what we own. More exists beneath the surface, beneath the superficial.

Continue to ponder this question: *What do we truly own?* Do we truly own our cars? We can purchase them and use them on our own terms, and we can assign a monetary value when we want to sell them. But if we truly *own* something, then that implies the existence of control. Do we totally control our cars? We think we do. We want to. But what if they break down on the highway? What if someone damages them? Can we prevent that? Or can we prevent natural wear and tear like corrosion and rust? Our cars, as with other material objects, are subject to the changing forces of nature. Even though we can drive our cars and take them wherever we would like, there are major aspects of them that we cannot control no matter how hard we try. Therefore, the idea that we can totally control something that we purchase and "own" is nothing but an illusion, a shadow on the back wall of the cave. We do not truly own our cars. It would be more accurate to say that we *borrow* our cars and use them while they last. With respect to control, our ownership of something has nothing to do with the fact that we purchased it. Purchasing something does not keep it from changing. To put it bluntly, when we buy a brand new car, don't we also buy the eventual demise of the car? So why get upset when it eventually fails to work properly?

Anything material is subject to change and deterioration, which we cannot control as much as we would like to *think* that we can. It is our illusory sense of *ownership* of an object that is often a source of discontent in our lives. When we *think* we own something, we often *expect* that change will not happen, that the car will always behave the way we want it to, that nobody can break it. And when something does not go our way, we get upset. Notice how a simple change in mindset toward something that we use everyday – our cars – can already serve as a wonderful example to point us in the direction of smoothing what Freemasons refer to as our "rough ashlars." The rough ashlar, or a rough stone, is a symbol of our ignorant states of mind. As Entered Apprentices, we are taught to use the common gavel as a symbolic tool to "divest our minds and consciences of all the vices and superfluities of life." We must work toward a better life and a better society by smoothing the rough ashlar of our minds in order to prepare it for the ultimate building project of developing our moral and spiritual edifices.

Does getting upset over something we cannot control do anything to help us? Not really. It's usually just a waste of calories. We often create more problems than we solve by becoming overly emotional. It is not that emotions are bad. Rather, it is the clutter of *unnecessary* emotions and our attachments to them that cloud our minds and often preclude us from our best judgment. Isn't such mental vexation that we impose on ourselves totally futile and superfluous? Yes! So let's chip that vice away with those gavels of ours. We become happier as a result of it; we benefit from our own efforts at divesting our minds of vices. It is not a rule or a moral, dogmatic conviction that is being imposed on us by the Entered Apprentice degree.

Rather, it is simply a better way to live. In this respect, we would be foolish to cling to our vices! Often, we only need to find the value behind a new way of life before we become willing to change. This is the primary challenge presented to the Entered Apprentice — to see life from a different perspective.

How about money? Is that something that we truly own? We have all heard that money isn't everything and that money cannot buy happiness. But let's think deeper. We absolutely cannot deny that money is powerful and that it can buy certain luxuries. A wealthy person is more able to perform charity, and businesses with more capital can invest in more stock. Happiness to a certain extent really is intertwined with financial security, regardless of the trite saying that money isn't everything. Thus, the rite of divesting in the Entered Apprentice degree does not refute the benefits of financial success. Rather, the Entered Apprentice degree calls our attention to the fact that money *comes* and *goes*. It is a *temporary* possession, just like any other material object that we may *think* we own. To seek happiness in the fleeting phenomenon of wealth would be as futile as chasing the flickering shadows in the cave. So who are we underneath our metallic coins? What do we truly own?

It is easy to speak of our material possessions as being unsatisfying and being of less value than wisdom, compassion, inner peace, and other philosophical ideals. But what about our views toward other people? What is another way we can think of our relationships? We can return to the same question posed by the symbolism of the Entered Apprentice degree. Do we own our friends? Do we own our significant others? If our friends, our girlfriends, or our wives are truly "ours," then we would be in control of them *at all times*. Is this the case?

Those who claim ownership or *think* that they own someone else will run into trouble. We may not openly say that we "own" another person, but intimate relationships often involve subconscious expectations that imply a level of control. As with our car analogy, control implies ownership. When we exert any form of control over a fellow human being, we are automatically going against his or her natural, innate ability and desire to think independently. This then carries into problems with respect, empathy, and communication that often plague social groups and the typical household. Sociologists, marriage counselors, and psychiatrists have spent careers trying to correct these issues. But oftentimes, the best therapy is *self-realization*, and a great way to begin is to ask ourselves, "What do we truly own?"

Through our discussion thus far, we have shown that we deceive ourselves when we consciously think about owning our material possessions or when we subconsciously think that we own our friends and companions. So what do we truly own? Clearly, it is nothing that resides solely in the external world around us. Where else can we look?

As we will learn in later degrees, Truth cannot be described with words. By definition, words are concepts, and they imply an imperfect description of reality. In pursuit of Truth and wisdom, it is often easier to begin by looking at what Truth is *not*, thereby narrowing the focus of our discussion. Likewise, in an attempt to find what we truly own, we have first discussed what we do *not* own. We have begun to learn that our inability to accept what lies behind the shadows is deeply rooted in our clinging to the false sense of ownership of objects, money, and people. This attachment is what brings us much deep-seated dissatisfaction in life. As we gradually lift the veil and see our surroundings and relationships more clearly, the effects of respect, success, and happiness will naturally follow, like a ray of light emanating from the sun.

Through the symbolism of the Entered Apprentice degree, we learn that we come into this world with nothing material, and we will leave it without being able to take anything material with us. This may seem like common sense at first, but are we truly living by this idea? Or is this just another thought that we try to cover up and file away for the sake of continuing to run in the hamster wheel? Coming to terms with, rather than avoiding, the facts of life will ultimately lead us on a happier and more satisfying life journey.

Understanding and accepting that all things change in life is not pessimistic, nor is it depressing. It is a *fact*, whether we want to accept it or not. It is realistic, not cynical, to accept change. For those of us who may feel that accepting the "hard truth" is depressing, think about it this way: by accepting something for what it is, have we lost anything? We do not deny the value of something just because we know it is not permanent. Seeing our cars as objects that may break at any time does not devalue them. Rather, it allows us to appreciate and cherish every moment we have behind the wheel! This realization leads us another step closer to the pot of gold at the end of our journey.

We *borrow* our time here on earth. We *borrow* our money. We *borrow* the land that we "own." We *borrow* the resources that we use. We *borrow* the time we can spend with our loved ones. Thinking this way, each moment is valuable. Each second is to be cherished. Each day is a gift.

CHARITY

As Entered Apprentices, we are taught the values of faith, hope, and charity. While all three values are important in their own ways, faith waxes and wanes like the phases of the moon as circumstances change in our lives. Likewise, hope may increase or decrease as we navigate the trials and travails of our journey. But the effects of charity continue onward beyond our realm of thought and vision. There is never a bad time to perform charity. When we help someone, either through the giving of tangibles, such as financial support, or the intangibles, such as friendship and trust, our acts of kindness extend well beyond the limits of those actions alone. Like a candle that shares its flame with other candles, the intensity of the light given by the first candle does not fade, and the light of the other candles continues even after the first candle is extinguished. Thus, charity should have a special place in every Mason's heart.

We have all heard the saying that we should learn to walk a mile in someone else's shoes. This is an expression of empathy – to know and to see from the perspective of another person. This is standard practice for anyone who seeks to solve conflicts, be they on the personal or global scales. But let's take this a step further. Given what we have learned from the Entered Apprentice degree, we understand that the fundamental equality of the human race comes not from the basis of sectarian religion or our national heritage; it comes from our fundamental destitution. We come into this world with nothing, and we leave it with nothing. All of our worldly possessions and worldly forms of wealth do not travel with us beyond our current realm of existence. So are we not fundamentally equal? When we realize this, we would not even need to walk a mile in a brother's shoes. We would simply realize that his shoes are no different than ours.

When we see those around us: our brothers, our sisters, our mothers, our fathers, our relatives, our friends, and even total strangers as our fundamental equals –

underneath our individual wealth, fame, and possessions – we acknowledge our fundamental destitution. When we see reality as it is, when we see that we do not truly own the things that we *think* define us, a natural feeling of compassion blossoms. We do not need to be taught that charity is good. We do not need to be guilt-tripped into thinking that we must donate our time and money to a particular organization. When we *see* that we really are not different from our brothers, our charitable tendencies will arise naturally. We each fight the hard fight, and the least we can do is to help each other on this journey. By helping others, we help ourselves. That realization opens our hearts and allows us to *want* to contribute to the relief of our fellow human beings by default. No coercion or even teaching is necessary. At that point, the primary mission of the Entered Apprentice degree would be complete.

THE SECRET OF SECRETS

One of the first questions that often plagues new initiates to Freemasonry is, "Why secrets?" I have witnessed some Masonic scholars say that they believe Freemasonry to be a genuine, secret organization in the historical sense, being that it was one of the first organizations to pass information through oral tradition in confidence. On the other hand, the more popular saying is that "Freemasonry is not a secret society, but rather a society with secrets." To the general public, the debate is exacerbated by the misperception of popular media and conspiracy enthusiasts who assert that Freemasons are harboring some deep, dark secret that can change the course of the world. The latter myth was addressed in the introduction of this book, whereas the debate over the status of Freemasonry as a "secret organization" seems to be grounded in nothing more than a difference in definition.

The presence of secrets alone does not render an organization a "secret society." Most organizations in the world necessarily keep some information private, such as membership rosters, contact information, and financial records. A true secret society forbids its members to reveal their association with the society, does not advertise its meetings, and current members must select or "tap" new members. There are many different types of secret societies, but they differ considerably from Freemasonry. Freemasons are free to discuss their membership status with the public. In fact, it is not unusual to drive down the highway and see squares and compasses stuck on car bumpers anywhere in the country or the world. The times and locations of Masonic lodge meetings are publicly advertised. Service and fundraising events are routinely held with banners, signs, and posters – hardly a sign of a secret society. Furthermore, in stark contrast to secret societies, Freemasons are forbidden to recruit members. Those who are interested in joining must petition and apply for membership, for reasons aforementioned in the introduction of this book.

If Freemasonry were supposed to be a secret society, it would be the worst kept secret in town. But, while Freemasonry is *not* a secret society, there is an element of secrecy with respect to the content and performance of the three degrees. The reasons for this are simple. Since the three Masonic degrees are designed to inspire the candidate, they serve as an *experience* that encourages him to be introspective and to apply the hidden meanings behind the symbols to his life in his own way. The best and most precious lessons are the ones that a man learns for himself, not ones that are simply given to him through the words of a lecture or a book. Thus, for the degrees to be most rewarding for the candidate, his experience must not be spoiled by details prematurely revealed by others. However, the meanings, the interpretations, and the philosophies of the degrees are open for discussion at any time. In fact, those are not to be kept secret, because what value would ideas such as charity and empathy have if they are not shared with as many people as possible?

There are other reasons for secrecy in Masonic degree work, ranging from the practical to the philosophical. Given the cultivation of brotherly love and the Masonic imperative that we reach out and help needy brothers whenever we are able, there is certainly incentive for non-Masons to take advantage of the trust that Masons give to each other. For example, when I moved to Hawai'i and was faced with the logistical nightmare of relocating from the mainland United States to an island in the middle of the tropical Pacific, brother Masons who were total strangers rushed to my assistance. To this day, I cannot thank the brothers enough for storing my boxes, driving me around the island to complete initial errands, and helping me process my car shipment. Little deeds of beneficence add up, and the trust that I was able to give to these brothers – whom I did not know beforehand – was more than I could ever hope to offer to total strangers outside of Freemasonry.

Examples like these are prevalent throughout Freemasonry, and the assurance of assistance in times of need is a much sought-after luxury. But this tenet of brotherly love is not a mandate. It comes from the mutual realization that, as inculcated in the lesson of destitution in the Entered Apprentice degree, we are all *in this together*. Because of people who may seek to undermine this trust by taking advantage of those who genuinely put in the effort of self-improvement, the Masonic tradition of identifying legitimate members through passwords and handshakes becomes necessary. This is not done for the elitism of knowing something that the public does not. Rather, it is a form of identification, like carrying a passport while traveling aboard.

Another reason for the presence of secrets in Masonic degrees is the practice of building trust. If I cannot keep something as simple and menial as a password or handshake secret, what is my word worth to you? Would you come to me for assistance during a time of need? Would you trust me with your personal feelings or problems? Probably not.

Through the *practice* of keeping secrets, no matter how superficial they are, the Entered Apprentice degree appeals to the candidate's *conscience*, with the penalty of the obligation – which is purely symbolic – being a clear warning against false or inappropriate speech. As Brother George Washington once said:

Labour to keep alive in your breast that little celestial fire called conscience.

Gossip can be one of the most damaging things to a person. When someone asks us to keep something secret, unless we are causing damage by doing so, we should always remain faithful to that trust. In a sense, the real secrets of Freemasonry are the secrets that brothers share with each other in confidence – details about their lives, their families, their problems, and their aspirations. It has been said that the real secret of Freemasonry is that there are no secrets. The details of Masonic ritual or degree work, if totally divulged, would not be particularly earth shattering. For those who find no value in the philosophical journey of improving oneself, none of the so-called "secrets" would bear any meaning.

A person who has never seen a stop sign would not understand the implied instruction. Likewise, combinations of letters in Russian would mean nothing to a person who does not speak Russian. Symbols themselves do not inherently have any value. It is the perceiver – the interpreter of those symbols – who ultimately assigns the values to them. For someone who finds no appreciation in viewing life as a journey of discovery and self-realization, the symbols and the secrets of Freemasonry would be totally meaningless. Thus, the real secret of life lies not outside but within us.

Freemasonry's greatest secret is the sense of personal joy and fulfillment that comes from successfully molding our rough ashlars. It is an ongoing process that has no end, but each step of the journey takes us to greater insights and wisdom. The symbol of a secret encourages us to seek the Truth for ourselves, and it emphasizes the importance of silence. As Brother Wolfgang Amadeus Mozart put it:

[T]o talk well and eloquently is a very great art, but that an equally great one is to know the right moment to stop.

Words cannot describe that skin-tingling feeling while witnessing a truly awe-inspiring sunset in the Sierra Nevada Mountains, that sense of accomplishment after looking back across the finish line at the end of a marathon, or that joy when our children utter their first words after months of anticipation. There is no substitute for these *experiences*. Likewise, when we encounter that personal contentment associated with the discovery of our own purpose in life, no words can possibly describe that. The greatest secret of all is a secret only because it cannot be uttered.

THE CARDINAL VIRTUES

For centuries, the cardinal virtues have been described as four elements that coincide with a moral life. Thus, the initiate into Freemasonry becomes familiar with the virtues of temperance, fortitude, prudence, and justice. Justice is perhaps most familiar to us, predominantly used in the context of law. Most simply, it is the notion of equality and fairness among the members of civilized society. The good are rewarded and the bad are punished in a way that is consistent and fair. However, for many people, "seeking justice" is equated with "seeking retribution." A clear distinction must be made. Justice is a noble ideal of fairness, whereas retribution comes from our inability to forgive. This inability to forgive ultimately brings much mental strife into our lives.

Fortitude, like justice, is a fairly simple concept to grasp. It is that inner strength of mind and determination that carries us through life's most difficult moments. Opposite to cowardice, it is what emboldens us to survive any pain or danger. On our journey, fortitude is that fixed mental purpose that we need in order to face our own faults, to acknowledge our imperfections, and to seek the welfare of others without compensation. It takes courage, it takes strength, and it takes honor to turn that flashlight back toward ourselves during moments of reflection as we hike the trail in the darkness of ignorance.

Prudence is our ability to regulate our lives through the employment of rational and logical thought, rather than passions and emotion. It is to think clearly and to solve problems without causing more in the meantime. Negative side effects to our actions often occur when our minds are clouded with anger, hatred, or greed. Prudence is that calm and clear state of mind – that torch of reason, which cuts through the darkness of night. Without it, the decisions we make for the future are often riddled with mistakes.

Temperance is that restraint of mind that keeps us from overindulging and engaging in extreme behaviors. While it is often used in modern times to describe the avoidance of drinking alcohol to excess, the word means much more. According to the Entered Apprentice degree, our first task as a Mason is to learn to quell our passions. And since emotions underlie our actions, by watching our thoughts and emotions carefully, we naturally keep our actions guarded as well. Thus, temperance includes the avoidance of anything, particularly actions that are habit forming, that may render our body or mind ungovernable. To break this first task of a Mason would be to overlook a crucial component of the Entered Apprentice degree. Yet the issue of temperance is a deeply personal one. It is up to the individual to define what doing something in moderation means. Anything that may cause an addiction, from alcohol to gambling, should be reduced or avoided before they become problems – the extent of which depends on the individual. Although no single person can unilaterally impose a particular standard on everyone, each individual brother is admonished to apply his best and most honest judgment to gauge and circumscribe himself.

All too frequently, the moral issues of temperance become intertwined with religious conviction until the practical reasons behind living a life of temperance become totally obscured. And for many people, this is why they throw out the issue all together and choose not to care. "But this is what's cool to do!" they say. Or, "Come on, don't be lame. Why should I care about temperance?" Sure, overindulgence in anything can lead us to questionable behavior, but rather than thinking about the issue of temperance as a *moral* one, why not think of it as a *practical* one that can actually lead us to a happier life?

It may initially seem counterintuitive to say that changing our idea of what's "fun" or what "makes me feel good" can lead us to greater happiness. But remember, the journey that we are on is to break free of our limited experiences in the cave and to see the wide expanse of the world outside. We should let go of our fears to question *certain* societal norms, such as what people *think* they need in order to "have fun" or to "be happy." When we do so, we begin to see what we have been missing all along.

The nature of addiction, however mild, rests in our mind's inability to operate on its own without something to keep it occupied. Those who are addicted to gambling find it hard to believe that anyone can have fun while sitting and chatting at a coffee shop. Likewise, someone who has made it a serious habit to party every weekend, probably will have a hard time relating to the excitement of a week-long backpacking trip in the middle of a mountain wilderness. On the other extreme, a person who only depends on coffee shops or constant backpacking trips in order to have fun loses touch with those who live a different lifestyle. So it is not that any particular activity is inherently good or bad. Rather, it is the degree to which our minds have become *governed by* those activities that is the real problem.

True happiness comes from our ability to control our minds and emotions. We think we do this on a day-to-day basis, but in reality, we let our emotions *control us* most of the time. In effect, by depending on an object or activity to keep us happy, we give up our ability to be happy without it. On the other hand, by liberating our minds from the shackles of what we *think* we need in order to be happy, we maximize our free will. To be happy and to be able to have fun *with* or *without* something – regardless of the circumstance – is true happiness. Thinking in this way, temperance no longer equates to "ruining the fun." In fact, the opposite is true; it gives us more mental freedom!

Freedom is not our ability to do whatever we want. Rather, true freedom is our ability to *let go* of the habits and emotions that hold us hostage in our mental prison cell, not because habits and emotions are bad, but because we do not know who we truly are underneath our complicated emotions and feelings. It is this confusion that drives the emotional rollercoaster that we *think* defines human life. But no, there is more – much more – outside the cave. By discussing the issue of temperance and looking outside the cave, it becomes less of a moral issue and more of a practical one. By understanding and controlling our passions, we acknowledge that the true nature of our mind exists without the need for anything external to constantly satisfy us. Because all external things constantly change with time, they will never be permanently satisfying! Instead, Freemasonry advises that we turn our attention inward.

So how do we find what is truly satisfying? Be patient, my brother. These are lessons we can only learn as we continue the journey toward that pot of gold. They must be your own personal realizations. I can offer to join you on the journey, but ultimately, we each must walk with our own two legs. For now, rest assured in the realization that temperance could be thought of as increasing our freedom, not limiting it.

So...back to the burning questions of the Entered Apprentice degree. What do we truly own? Who are we? A Mason and retired U.S. Naval veteran in Oklahoma once told me, "Find out who you are. Don't worry about anything else for now. Just find out who you are. The moment you find out, your table will be set before you." Let's keep walking.

III

The Checkered Pavement

As we embark on our Masonic journey, we look around and notice that we stand on a checkered pavement: a floor pattern tiled with black and white squares. Resembling a chessboard, this mosaic that is familiar to all Masons is more than just an 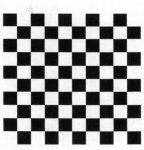 ornament in lodge. It is a deeply profound, philosophical symbol.

The story of the Entered Apprentice degree describes the checkered pavement as a representation of the lowest floor of King Solomon's Temple. Much of the allegory and symbolism of the Masonic degrees traditionally comes from the Old Testament of the Holy Bible, with a special emphasis on the Temple of King Solomon. However, it is imperative that we keep in mind that these are only *symbols* and are not meant to be historical accounts or signs of religious endorsement. They are meant to encourage us to seek the deeper, philosophical meanings that reside behind the veil of allegory. Such a mindset opens up a wealth of potential wisdom.

When we stand on the checkered pavement, we notice that the black and white colors represent our tendencies to divide everything around us into opposing categories. Our minds *conceptualize* what is around us, and in order to make sense of our surrounding world, we apply artificial divisions to all that we observe. This is an attempt by our consciousnesses to simplify the world around us, but in doing so, we fall into the trap of thinking that our simplification is how life really is. We confuse the projection on the classroom wall for the actual document. We confuse the *concept* for what is *real*.

We have all heard the saying that life is not black and white. But are we truly applying this wisdom? Once again, we find a common disconnect between the wisdom of a familiar idiom and our day-to-day actions. This is where our journey comes into play. Let's work toward understanding more fully what it means to truly live by the idea that life is not black and white.

Is water good or bad for you? Pause for a second to think about this question before continuing to read. This is perhaps the best and simplest illustration of our tendencies to overly conceptualize reality into black and white categories. Let's play this mental game and see what the checkered pavement is trying to teach us.

Of course, water is good! Water is the most unique, life-sustaining element on earth. Life as we know it owes its existence to the presence of water, which possesses unique chemical properties that set it apart from all other chemical elements on earth. If it were not for the fact that upon freezing, the density of water *decreases* during its phase transition from liquid to solid, ice would not float on the surface of lakes in the winter, fresh water fish and other aquatic life would freeze, and higher life forms would be severely affected. For these reasons, water is clearly a good thing. But can water also be bad? Of course! Countless numbers of people drown each year around the world, either through water-related accidents or weather-induced flooding that can destroy entire communities. On the other hand, torrential rains can reinvigorate our farms during a drought.

So is water good or bad? Perhaps it is both good *and* bad? But how can something be simultaneously composed of opposite characteristics? That does not logically make any sense. Water that drowns someone obviously is not both good *and* bad; it's just totally bad! Water that enters a dehydrated person's body is not both good *and* bad; it's completely good!

Clearly, we have identified a paradox. What is the inherent nature of water? Perhaps a better answer would be: It *depends*. Ah! Here, we begin to approach the true answer. The reality of water is neither inherently good, inherently bad, nor simultaneously both. So the question of whether something is good or bad is *flawed*. Remember our statement from our earlier discussion that "nothing is inherently anything?" Well, simply observing the nature of water can teach us this very important lesson. Water is just water. It just *is*. It *is* the way it *is*. No further description or concept is necessary. In fact, using any adjective would be limiting what it really *is*.

Let's use some other examples to further illustrate this *principle of non-duality*. For those in the military, are orders from commanding officers always good or always bad? Well, they are good if the orders are issued as part of a successful plan toward the completion of a mission. But what if a particular officer abuses his leadership position by injecting personal bias in an attempt to benefit himself rather than the mission? In that case, the order would not be good. As with water, whether a military order is good or bad *depends* on the situation.

For those who are scientifically minded, is light made of particles or waves? In the early development of quantum physics, light was determined to have different qualities, *depending* on the circumstance. The different colors of visible light were determined to be a result of the interference between light waves of different wavelengths and frequencies. This interference could not be explained by particles, so scientists used this as evidence that light exists as waves. But under proper measurement conditions, light acts as a stream of photons, or light particles, consisting of individualized packets of energy. This is evidence that counters the wave theory. So is light ultimately a wave or a particle? Even in the materialistic and mathematical study of the sciences, we see the manifestation of the principle of non-duality. Both waves and particles are nothing more than concepts, so the true nature of light *transcends* both the concepts that we impose upon it.

For those who prefer a religious example, is faith good or bad? Typically, the concept of faith is showered with praise and even serves as a cornerstone in most religious traditions. But to illustrate the universal nature of non-duality, we can analyze this concept further. For a person who clings to faith to bring him out of the depths of depression, drug addiction, or serious illness, faith is a great thing! But what if certain individuals wreak havoc and terrorize the masses in the name of faith for their particular beliefs? In this case, faith loses its noble qualities. So what is the true nature of faith?

We can continue this exercise as we go about our daily lives. Although the checkered pavement was introduced to us within a Masonic lodge, the lessons and philosophies embedded within this symbol can and should be universally applied outside of lodge. As part of our journey, we can begin to practice this principle of non-duality by identifying things in our daily lives that we habitually break into artificial black and white categories. Once we understand this ignorant, subconscious habit of ours, we can begin to turn it around and simply see the realities behind all phenomena for what they are. We can then act in accordance to a mindset that is free from the illusion of duality. There are never only two options. There are never only two courses of action.

While this discussion may at first seem like nothing more than philosophical gibberish, it is actually very practical. If we can prove to ourselves the non-duality of all phenomena, then we have traveled one step closer to understanding life beyond the shadows in the cave. Immediately, we would see practical applications in daily life that would improve our interpersonal relationships. Like water, we should see our friends, our family, our colleagues, and our supervisors for who they are, not for who we *think* they are. Sounds simple, right? Well, not really, because if we all truly lived by this philosophy, there would be no misunderstandings between people, and respect and empathy would allow no room for false judgment. But unfortunately, in addition to our habitual problem of conceptualization, our egos chain us to our own beliefs, taking those concepts to be absolute and irrefutable. Furthermore, it is very difficult to break free from the chains of ego. This is why the application of these philosophies must take *practice*. This is why we speak of this process of self-improvement as nothing less than a journey.

When we let go of our notion of something or someone always *being* a particular adjective – a concept – then we free ourselves to acknowledge all the possibilities. If we view our long-time friend as a static object that never changes, we would be sorely disappointed when he changes his mind against our will. If we view someone who wronged us in the past as an inherently terrible person, then we completely ignore the possibility of his eventual change in heart and deprive him of the joy of redemption. By locking in a particular adjective for someone, we go against the very nature of the truth of change. So why not acknowledge and embrace the fact that nothing is set in stone?

As with everything in life, we do not deny that water really is good or that water really is bad *in certain situations*. Realism is not denial. In fact, the opposite is true. By attaching ourselves to artificial concepts and dualistic categories, we are denying ourselves the truth. If we embrace reality, rather than ignore it, we liberate our minds and begin to live a happier life. Otherwise, we ignore all the possibilities, and thus, we generate misunderstandings; we attach ourselves to things of which we should let go; we hate the things that we need to forgive; and we deprive ourselves of inner peace.

THE ILLUSION OF OUR PLACE IN DUALITY

A natural side effect of dualistic thought is *judgment*. When we divide the world around us into black and white categories, we automatically place ourselves in one of those categories. Immediately, our division of black and white results in the problem of *me* versus *you*. Through judgment, we alienate ourselves from the rest of the world or from a particular group. We tear each other apart. Like throwing a pebble in the water and generating ripples that propagate outward, our dualistic thoughts create judgments that generate a wave train of emotions that perpetuate our daily rollercoaster of vexations.

The issue of good versus evil is a wonderful example of this. Regardless of what our particular religious faiths may say about good and evil, we must realize that oftentimes even the definitions of good and evil are subjective. What one culture may consider good, another may consider evil. Likewise, what is banned by one country may be easily accepted in another. Who is correct? It's an unanswerable question, much like the question of whether water is good or bad. It *depends*.

So without delving into the *essence* of good and evil, because that is in the domain of religion, let's just think about how we can adjust our mindsets so that our view of the world does not hinder our progress on the journey toward wisdom. Regardless of our beliefs – which we have every right to keep – we should learn to let go of the notion that we are always correct. Even if we don't agree with another viewpoint, we should at least accept that both sides exist as a byproduct of conceptualizations. This acceptance breeds respect and is a sign of humility.

We often hear in religious sermons that we should not judge others. But why is such a simple teaching so difficult to follow? It is because the ultimate root of our problem lies not in the judgment itself but in our habitual division of everything into black and white. When we think of the world as nothing but a struggle between good and evil, we naturally take sides and pass judgment. However, a wise and compassionate person who understands "good" will not judge others, because part of being "good" is to let go of the selfish ego. A true scientist, upon making a major discovery, will not brag about his accomplishment. Instead, as with Albert Einstein when he formulated his theory of relativity, the true scientist pours his heart out and is overwhelmed with humility upon the realization of how little he really knows. A truly good person will live in total humility and will lead by example, rather than tear others down with judgment.

To successfully address the issue of false judgment, we must dig deeper and confront our dualistic thoughts. Take a look at this picture. What do you see? Do you see a white vase? Or do you see two black faces? Without the white vase, we would not be able to see the black faces.

Without the black faces, the white vase would not exist. The full picture contains *both*. In fact, the existence of *either* the vase or the faces depends on the *mutual* existence of both! One arises simultaneously with the other. In this picture, neither the vase nor the faces can exist independently. Such is the irony of good and evil. Although they are on different ends of the spectrum, the fact that they *are* opposites implies that they must – by definition – coexist. If you were asked the length of the table in front of you, would you be able to answer without using a ruler or some relative unit of measurement? No. So all definitions are *relative*, because they must *depend* on something else as a measure. Darkness is merely the absence of light. Thus, to say that one side of the coin must defeat the other would be a ludicrous breakdown of logic. Rather, an all-loving, pure, and compassionate state of being transcends *both* incomplete pictures and understands that Truth goes well beyond this illusion of duality.

This same principle of non-duality is true for all the other thoughts and emotions that we use to conceptualize the world around us. A similar dilemma exists in the realm of love and hate. We often think of love and hate as extreme opposites. But how often do extreme love and infatuation lead to hatred because it is not returned? When we love our significant other so much that we can't bear to live without her, and that love is somehow shot down, our love can quickly turn into hatred. On the other hand, it was the extreme hatred of the Nazi soldiers that inspired the most selfless acts of love from Jewish neighbors to help each other in the concentration camps. Think of your family. I bet that, as with most families, there have been moments of affection and good times, but also moments of extreme difficulty. For many, the most agonizing and difficult moments in life are related to family conflicts, yet families originate with love. Conversely, the strongest of love can heal the toughest of wounds. Such is the nature of love and hate. Are they really that far apart? Or are they both only separated by a fine line, like the vase and the faces in the optical illusion?

By realizing the true nature of dualities, we diminish nothing. We still acknowledge and value love for what it is, but instead of selfish love, we begin to embrace *compassion*, which is unconditional. Compassion is the ultimate form of love, because it is driven by empathy rather than a desire for self-gratification. By seeing the big picture, we free ourselves from the shackles of disappointment in the face of events we cannot control. In the end, we cherish the moments of joy and can muster the mental stamina to endure the most difficult of challenges, for these dualities are simply parts of the same grand picture of life.

If reality does not follow our subjective categorizations, and if our feelings, judgments, and actions are based upon these illusory concepts, then are we not habitually taking the shadows in the cave for what is real? We see now what is meant by the symbol of our perpetual state of darkness in the Entered Apprentice degree. If everything we feel, everything we judge, and everything we do is based on our *impressions* and our own *opinions* of the world around us, are we not technically living in a dream of our own creation? And when the bubble of our dream bursts, we get upset. So are we not the authors of our own mental anguish? Conversely, we have the exact same ability to be authors of our own mental happiness, which brings us tremendous hope. But first, we must wake up from our dream. We must learn to see past our limited perspectives and see life for what it really is. When we wake up from our illusion of duality, we become more in tune with our colleagues, we become closer friends with our peers, we become more compassionate in our relationships, and we make wiser decisions even in the most difficult of circumstances. In short, our lives become better.

INTERDEPENDENCE

Our discussions lead us to another lesson of the Entered Apprentice degree. In our state of darkness, we act like a person who is blindfolded and requires a guide to lead him in the right direction. Even as we vow to seek light, exactly where we should look remains a mystery. During our travels, we must depend on other people. This dependence underscores another major lesson in our journey toward light: all things are connected. We are all interdependent.

The reason that water cannot be described with specific adjectives like "good" or "bad" is that water does not exist independently of *causes* and *conditions*. When asked about whether water is good or bad, we answered, "It depends." With this answer, we acknowledge the fact that all things must depend on certain conditions. An apple seed that is planted must be given proper light, water, and nutrients in order for it to grow. Likewise, all things in life are conditioned phenomena. They require a network of interconnected processes in order to exist.

When we wake up in the morning, we perform our usual routine: shower, brush our teeth, eat breakfast, and then drive to work. Where did the shampoo come from? Who made the plumbing that transports water? How was the toothbrush designed and delivered? Who made the toothpaste? How many farmers and ranchers went into growing and providing the food that is on our breakfast plates? How many factory workers assisted in the manufacturing of our cars? Who drilled and processed the oil that eventually became the gasoline in our gas tanks? In just the brief period of time from our morning alarm to our commute to work, we have to make use of the services of how many hundreds, thousands, or even tens of thousands of people? Without the inconceivably large network of people who indirectly contribute to our daily lives, civilization as we know it would cease to exist.

When we truly understand the interdependent nature of life, how can we possibly find time to complain about anything? When we see other people as extremely valuable elements in the web of life, compassion and empathy would be nothing but natural states of mind. When we see ourselves as an indelible part of the universe, we strive to do our best to make this world a better place. We realize that there is absolutely no time to waste on selfish aims. A house cannot stand strong with one brick missing, so let's do our part to contribute to a strong and prosperous society. Life is not just about personal satisfaction. It is about the miracle of the web of interdependence. This alone should inspire us to leave behind our petty differences, our personal desires, and our attachments to our own egos.

Earlier, the will to perform charity came from the realization that a candle can share its flame with countless other candles without diminishing its own light. Now, we take that a step further and see that the wisdom of interdependence comes from the realization that by lighting other candles, we benefit ourselves by increasing the total, ambient light in the room. By sharing more, we obtain more. By giving, we receive. With this understanding, the specter of greed and selfishness naturally dissolves. There is no need to suppress anything. There is no need to work toward anything. Simply change the mind, and actions will follow.

We have learned much on our journey thus far. But there are more rivers to ford, forests to conquer, and mountains to climb. What once appeared to be a seemingly impossible expedition now becomes a rewarding journey. We are walking the trail less traveled. Indeed, not many have journeyed this way with us. Even among those who have, few have taken the time to stop, question, and smell the sweet fragrance of the pine trees. The vivid colors of the wildflowers, the glory of the blue sky, and the peaceful hum of the dragonflies have often passed with little notice. But now – now we have learned to embrace the full *experience*. Only through experience do we truly live. Come. Let us continue.

What's that up ahead? Hmm...that's odd. Looks like a flight of stairs.

IV

The Climb

As we continue our Masonic journey, we cannot help but notice the prominence of the two pillars located at the entrance of King Solomon's Temple, as mentioned in the Holy Bible. Large and imposing, like two sequoia trees flanking our trail, these towering pillars symbolize an important aspect of our journey. They remind us of the importance of living a life devoid of extremes. Though we enjoy the pleasurable, too much of one thing is never good. On the contrary, extreme self-deprivation and asceticism lead us nowhere. A guitar string that is too loose will not make a sound, but one that is too tight will snap. The string must be perfectly in tune in order to produce the most beautiful melodies and harmonies. Likewise, our journey to light requires us to walk *between* the two pillars.

As a Fellow Craft, we are taught the names of the two pillars. Although many different synonyms exist, one particular interpretation is that they represent "power" and "responsibility." Although these seem to be totally unrelated, careful inspection proves otherwise.

Power is that characteristic of strength that enables us to conquer the odds. Physically, power is the ability to lift heavy objects, run a marathon, perform major construction projects, and accelerate quickly on a highway. Mentally, power is represented by our ability to make proper decisions, withstand irrational criticism, serve as a good leader, and exhibit the virtues of inner strength. But both physical and mental power can be highly detrimental.

Power can be used to conquer, to make unjustified war, to take advantage of others, and to feed our egos.

Responsibility is the result of a mind that acts with restraint, control, and compassion. It is the foremost characteristic of a good person, and those who act responsibly are sure to win the respect of all – a sign of an effective leader. To be responsible is to see and fully understand the consequences of all of our actions. It is seeing the future with proper foresight. It is the foundation of civilized society. But it alone has its limitations.

Responsibility is a passive trait, whereas power is an active one. Without power, a responsible and compassionate person can only be of little good. But without responsibility, power can be destructive. The two characteristics depend on each other. Responsibility without power is weak. Power without responsibility can devastate. A good life involves a journey that lies in between these two qualities. A proper balance is essential. This can easily be related to the cardinal virtues in the Entered Apprentice degree. Power underscores *fortitude* and enforces *justice*, whereas responsibility is a sign of *prudence* and *temperance*. The Spider Man's uncle, Ben Parker, best summarized the balance between the two pillars, "With great power," he said, "comes great responsibility."

THE SPIRAL STAIRCASE

I thought I caught a glimpse of it earlier from the trail, and it now looks like I'm right; there's a spiral staircase just up ahead. Looks like it's a bit overgrown with shrubs and bushes, but we can manage. It has to lead somewhere, right? Since our expedition would not be an adventure otherwise…let's climb it!

Before we take our first steps, we must remember that no matter where we go or what we climb, we must do the walk ourselves. Nobody can do it for us. Even if we have a trusted friend who can guide us for a while, we must still climb and work up a sweat or else we deprive ourselves of the lessons that come with the *experience*. The Entered Apprentice degree challenged us to *see* beyond our limited perspectives. Now, the Fellow Craft degree challenges us to *learn* and to *practice*. We have no time to waste. Let's start the climb and see what we find!

As we begin our ascent, we notice the curved nature of the spiral staircase – a perfect symbol for our life journey. Oftentimes, our paths are not simple and direct, but rather, difficult and winding. We cannot see what is right around the corner. There is no way of predicting the events that may occur in our lives next year, next week, tomorrow, or even in the next minute. We make goals. We plan. We organize. But at the end of the day – or shall we say, at the end of *this moment* – we have no idea exactly what will happen next. What is right around the corner? Perhaps it is a surprise raise in our paycheck. Or perhaps we will be laid off without warning.

We can and should prepare for the future, but we lack the element of control when we look forward into the distance. At the same time, we should not be afraid of the unknown that lies just around the corner. Fear is but another fleeting emotion that we need to acknowledge but let go, for being afraid will not help us with the situation at hand. Instead, let's *cherish* what we currently have. When we understand the fragility of life, each day is precious. Moment by moment, we are receiving a gift. It is our responsibility to figure out what we want to do with each of those gifts.

The view continuously gets better the higher we climb. We begin to see the elements of our lives more clearly. Those things that we once took for granted, we begin to appreciate. We temporarily step outside of our egos and give thanks to what we have grown accustomed. We express gratitude for the things that we have wrongly assumed would always be there. We see more clearly the support that our friends gave us during times of need. We respect the wisdom of our early schoolteachers, who gave us their patience when we were throwing paper airplanes around the classroom. We acknowledge the incredible love and care of our parents. Even if our childhoods or later adult lives were riddled with family problems, the pain and uncertainty that we imposed on our mothers during and after the moments of our births deserve wholehearted thanks, regardless of later events in life. Our current existence alone is reason enough to give thanks to our parents. As we climb higher and see the bigger picture, we learn to give thanks to all the people who have contributed to our current state of being. This is the practice of *compassion*.

As we climb even higher, we look down and notice that we leave behind the checkered pavement. We rise above it. We *transcend* it. We go beyond the realm of dualistic thought. The higher we climb, the more we see. We see the full picture for what it *is*, not just the little, individual boxes of black and white. We see the *entire* mosaic. We see each of the boxes as merely parts of the same *whole*. Up here, the air is fresher, the breeze is comforting, and the view is breathtaking. Brother Rudyard Kipling described this transcendence of the realm of dualities in his famous poem, "If." An excerpt appears in the Wimbledon's Centre Court players' entrance, and Roger Federer and Rafael Nadal recited the poem in a 2008 promotional video:

If you can keep your head when all about you
Are losing theirs and blaming it on you;
If you can trust yourself when all men doubt you,
But make allowance for their doubting too;
If you can wait and not be tired by waiting,
Or, being lied about, don't deal in lies,
Or, being hated, don't give way to hating,
And yet don't look too good, nor talk too wise;

If you can dream — and not make dreams your master;
If you can think — and not make thoughts your aim;
If you can meet with Triumph and Disaster
And treat those two imposters just the same;
If you can bear to hear the truth you've spoken
Twisted by knaves to make a trap for fools,
Or watch the things you gave your life to broken,
And stoop and build 'em up with worn out tools;

If you can make one heap of all your winnings
And risk it on one turn of pitch-and-toss,
And lose, and start again at your beginnings
And never breathe a word about your loss;
If you can force your heart and nerve and sinew
To serve your turn long after they are gone,
And so hold on when there is nothing in you
Except the Will which says to them: "Hold on !";

If you can talk with crowds and keep your virtue,
Or walk with kings — nor lose the common touch;
If neither foes nor loving friends can hurt you;
If all men count with you, but none too much;
If you can fill the unforgiving minute
With sixty seconds' worth of distance run —
Yours is the Earth and everything that's in it,
And — which is more — you'll be a Man my son!

By the pillars and the spiral staircase, we realize that the true wisdom of life lies in the perfection of avoiding extremes *and* the transcendence of dualities. Such a mind is free from bias, free from judgment, and free from contempt. The next step would be to free it from the chains of ego, which will come later in our journey. In the meantime, in addition to an increase in gratitude, we see and acknowledge our faults and shortcomings because we must realize our mistakes before we can fix them. When we look back at the checkered pavement and view our initial, limited perspectives – our initial state of darkness – we realize the futility of our situation prior to the journey. We start to understand that there is truly more to life outside of the cave.

Although our perspectives from the spiral staircase are vastly improved, our vision of what lies ahead still remains limited. We still do not know what is waiting for us just around the corner. The spiral staircase requires faith of what is to come. We do not know what we will find near the top of the climb, but until we can experience our own answers, we must trust those who have gone before us. We trust their words when they say, "The journey was worth it." Although personal, first-hand experience is a necessity, we must also rely on the wisdom of those who have gone before. By having faith in those who deserve our trust, we guarantee a worthwhile and useful supplement to our own experiences. As with power and responsibility, personal experience and wisdom learned from others must be balanced. This is the task of a Fellow Craft.

LIVING IN THE PRESENT MOMENT

An intriguing aspect of climbing any flight of spiral staircases is the relative difficulty of taking each of the steps, compared to a normal flight of stairs. If we are not careful or if we are not paying attention, we can easily trip and fall. Instead, we must be ever mindful of the present moment and concentrate on our immediate steps. As Brother Franklin Delano Roosevelt asserted:

The only limit to our realization of tomorrow will be our doubts of today.

Let me share a personal story. When I lived in Oklahoma, Brother Daniel Herr, one of my best friends from college, came to visit. Since I was a meteorologist involved with tornado field research, we traveled the Plains during that week in search of the most devastating storms on earth. After observing a few tornadoes, the excitement waned, and the return of fair weather guaranteed relative boredom in the Plains. Dan and I were both avid outdoorsmen; so naturally, we tried to find a suitable outdoor activity in which to partake. But there were no mountains to hike in central Oklahoma, and the usual forms of entertainment found in big cities or major parks in other areas of the country were virtually nonexistent.

One day, Dan asked me to join him on a bike ride through my low-key town of Norman. "Where do you want to go?" I asked. Norman was a college town – home of the Sooners – but compared to the mountains of northern California where Dan was from, it was devoid of any major form of outdoor recreation much beyond hunting and fishing. I was a bit surprised by Dan's request to go cycling. "Unless you want to go all the way out to Lake Thunderbird, which does not even come close to Lake Tahoe where you're from…there's no place to go here besides maybe some city parks with picnic tables," I insisted.

"So what? Does it matter?" Dan responded, looking at me with a slight hint of consternation.

"Well, then where do you want to go?" I asked again, not finding it worthwhile to go anywhere in Norman without a purpose.

"I don't know," he said casually, not seeming to care about my concern.

"So, do you want to pack a lunch or something? Maybe do a picnic at a nearby park? Or maybe we can check out the area by the small airport on the north side of town?" I suggested, trying to come up with some purpose for the bike ride.

Dan simply turned and walked out with a bicycle in the garage. "You coming or not?" he asked.

Well, considering he was the guest, it would have been totally unbecoming of me as the host not to have at least tried my best to entertain, so I dropped my doubts and decided to tag along. "Alright, fine," I accepted reluctantly, "but don't say I didn't warn you that there's nothing to see around here compared to where you're from!"

And so, we started our bike ride to − nowhere in particular. We followed a road north through town, sped through several puddles left by the rain shower earlier in the day, and took turns in the lead. We made it to the northern outskirts of town near a municipal airport and tested our skills in tackling mud puddles on our mountain bikes. A fan of extreme sports, Dan told me about the mountain bike course that he and his brother built. We talked about the injuries that came with practicing stunts − as I watched Dan take his bike down a flight of stairs in front of an abandoned building by the airport. We then discussed the details of our lives since we graduated from college, stories from childhood, and our hopes for the future.

After a blitz down Main Street, we took another break, and I practiced some basic jumps on the bike over the curbs in an empty parking lot. Then, we explored unfamiliar roads and parts of town to which I had never been. I was fascinated by the various convenience stores, small businesses, churches, and unfamiliar schools that were tucked away in the humble corners of town. Dan spoke about a stunt that he once did on his bike, where he rode on the top of an elevated wall-like structure that was extremely narrow. Although he acknowledged the significant risks involved, his reason for telling the story came across loud and clear. "It was such a good form of mental training," he said. "When you are faced with such a difficult task, you can train yourself to just pay attention to each moment. You'd be surprised at what the human body can do. It's the mind that holds us back, not the body. And an experience like that, for me, is just awesome."

After over two hours of riding around town, we returned to my house. With our clothes covered in mud and our helmets dripping in sweat, we laughed and joked as we washed our bikes in the backyard. Between the new sights, the good conversation, and the cool breeze on my face, I had completely forgotten about why we went on the bike ride in the first place! And yet, I enjoyed every moment of it. I soaked in all the nuances of sight and sound. I learned things about the City of Norman that I did not know before. Although we were already good friends, through our conversation during the bike ride, I learned even more about who Dan was as a person and how that fit with his life goals. But most importantly, I learned about myself. I learned about my habits. I learned about my usual mindset. I learned about what I was and was not capable of doing. I learned about my reactions to new places and new ideas. I learned to challenge myself, not physically, but mentally…all within the space of two hours during a random bike ride around town.

The next day, we had lunch before I had to take Dan to the airport to catch his return flight. We reviewed all the great things we did that week, including the tornadoes we had seen and my memorable 24th birthday party. As we finished our meals, during a break in conversation, Dan looked at me and said, "Because you didn't know where you were *supposed* to go, you never would have gone on that bike ride, huh." I let out a sigh, grinned, and gave a slight nod.

On our way to the Oklahoma City airport, I finally began to realize some of what I had learned through the bike ride, although the significance of those lessons would not hit me until years later. "People are so strongly attached to their goals in life that they completely miss out on the journey," Dan said to me in the car. "Goals are good to have and all, but when we sacrifice *so much* just so that we can get something, when we don't even know if that *thing* is really what we need or want in life, then what are we doing? We're living for a dream but not really living." As I drove into the airport departures area, Dan summarized his message with these words:

If instead of concerning yourself with the score of the game, you concentrate your whole-hearted efforts on doing the best that you possibly can in your role that moment, regardless of your task — living in that moment, that minute, that second — when it comes to the end of the game, you will have achieved more and scored more than you previously thought possible.

As a high school basketball coach, these were the words that he conveyed to his team. I immediately realized that the "game" is not only limited to basketball, but also the "game of life" must be played in this way. Like that bike ride, not only is life a journey, but also to understand the true value, purpose, and reward of the journey, we must focus on the beauty of each second – moment by moment. The value of life lies in the means to the end, not the end. It is important to set goals, but to think that any one goal will be totally and permanently satisfying would be to live within the confines of our cave. Due to the natural passage of time, a goal, once reached, exists only for a moment, only to pass and become just another episode of our life journey. If we do not find value in our journey toward our goals, then how can we expect to find value in just the goals alone? An Olympic gymnast not only strives for the gold, but he must also love the sport and the training itself.

"Thank you," I said, at a total loss of how exactly to respond to the realization that had just dawned on me. As we stepped outside the car, I was overwhelmed with gratitude, "Dude, thank you so much for everything that you've taught me, whether you know it or not."

Dan chuckled and responded, "No, it's all you buddy, it's all you." He turned and walked into the airport terminal.

Although Dan was already going through his Masonic degrees, I was not yet a Mason at the time. But after having this epiphany and these moments of inspiration, it did not take me long to petition Norman Lodge No. 38 for membership. I would embark on my own Masonic journey later that summer.

While we can use Masonic symbolism to teach us about life, let this example of mine show that our life philosophies should not depend only on the *organization* of Freemasonry. Rather, the journey we are on is deeply personal. We do not have to be a Mason in order to improve ourselves, but for those of us who are members, it is a convenient way to keep us on the right track. We get out what we put in. For those who do not try to apply symbolism to their daily lives, no amount of work in lodge will lead them from darkness to light. Just because we hear something during a degree that is conferred to us does not mean that we are all of a sudden a better or more enlightened person. We must put it to *practice*. That is why Freemasonry is often referred to as a "craft." In the words of Bruce Lee:

Knowing is not enough, you must apply; willing is not enough, you must do.

Many thanks go to Brother Herr for inspiring me to start my Masonic journey, but more importantly, for helping me *realize for myself* that my entire life is nothing but a journey. Even the goals that we establish, once reached, simply come and go. They are but parts of the constant flow of experiences, like the trees that pass as we walk a trail through the forest. And it is up to us to figure out these lessons for ourselves. Nobody can do it for us. Nobody can teach these lessons to us. The most anybody can do is to set up the proper conditions for us to make our *own* realizations. As Dan said, "It's all you." He never *taught* me anything. He merely set me up to *learn for myself*. No amount of lecturing would have taught me to see life as a journey. As many times as I had heard the saying, "the journey is the reward," I still did not live by it. I had to experience it for myself. Nobody can ever impose their beliefs on anyone else, even if they think those beliefs are justified. Instead, by leading through example and setting up the necessary conditions for enlightened thought, people will naturally *see* for themselves the biggest lessons in life. And when they *see* for themselves, they truly *learn*.

When we climb the spiral staircase, we must *focus on the moment*, or else it is easy to trip and fall. We must *live in the moment* in order to fully concentrate on the task at hand.

This is true of all of our endeavors. However, we must emphasize an extremely important distinction. To live *in* the moment is not the same as to live *for* the moment! Please do not confuse these two statements! Often, there is great confusion between these two concepts. Upon hearing the philosophy that we should live *in* the moment, some people may think that the future does not matter so they can do whatever they want to fulfill their desires and pleasures *right now*. No! That would be living *for* the moment. Nothing can be further from the truth! When we live *for* the moment, we completely neglect the natural laws of cause and effect in our lives. We delude ourselves into thinking that by doing whatever we want right now, we would not have to suffer the potential consequences in the future. That would be nearsighted ignorance, not wisdom. On the other hand, to fully live *in* the moment is to *see* the reality of each moment in our lives more clearly – including all the causes, conditions, and consequences of our actions. In effect, we become more *aware* of our inner and outer worlds. Since our futures hinge on the present moment, if our inner thoughts are wise, then our actions are wise. When our actions are wise, our futures are filled with hope.

As we climb our journey, let's constantly practice the art of living in the present moment. When we are driving a car, drive. When we are walking on the street, walk. When we are writing a letter, write. When we are listening to a friend, listen. No matter what we are doing, we must always *pay attention* and reduce our extraneous distractions. To truly live in the moment is to pay full attention to what is going on. When we are fully *aware*, we become more capable of doing even our most routine tasks. Why do we sometimes forget where we put our keys or where we leave our wallets? These things happen when we are not *paying attention* to everything that we do. By focusing on the present moment and concentrating on one task and one task alone, we actually give our minds a break. As a result of that attentiveness, we perform the task better and improve our interpersonal relationships.

To be in full concentration might sound tedious at first, but it can be thought of as a more natural state of mind. We have simply become locked into the habit of thinking, daydreaming, and burying ourselves each day in unnecessary emotions like anger and frustration. We are constantly riding an exhausting rollercoaster, and we don't even know it! Why is it that we sometimes can't sleep at night? We have all experienced nights when our thoughts and emotions run wild. If these mental vexations were our natural states of mind, why would we not be able to sleep? So let's give ourselves a mental break every once in a while. Our physical bodies cannot be constantly running a marathon. Likewise, our minds cannot be constantly riding a rollercoaster of emotions without falling into a form of mental exhaustion. This exhaustion translates to stress, frustration, and our inability to cope with life in the face of uncontrollable circumstances. Here lies the essence of the admonition that all Masons have heard, that we should keep our passions and emotions within acceptable boundaries.

At the end of the day, being able to focus on the present moment can become one of our most valuable life skills. While goals are good and memories are valuable, we cannot let our dreams for the future or our nostalgia for the past keep us from focusing on our current step. When we are playing a sport during a competition, we must focus on putting forth our best effort. There is no room in our minds for "what ifs" or "this needs to happen or else..." All those thoughts merely distract us and preclude us from doing our best. Climbing our journey on the spiral staircase requires our full concentration and devotion to each step we take. The past is intangible. The future is intangible.

Even the present is intangible with respect to concepts, because the moment we say the word "present," that instant has already passed. Rather than getting caught up in words or semantics, let's simply *focus* on the *now*.

All of this is certainly easier said than done. Try sitting quietly by yourself for five minutes and think about nothing but your breath. Try it. I bet after only a short while, you will either begin to think of the past or dream about the future, what you did last night, or what you're about to make for lunch. We do this 99% of the time. We dream when we sleep, but we often also dream when we are awake, because we are usually thinking about the past or the future. These extraneous thoughts while we are talking, walking, driving, or working are not more real than the dreams we have when we are asleep. How much more efficient could our minds be if we were to simply focus on the tasks at hand without wasting mental resources on the intangible? When we ignore the reality of the present moment, are we not living in a dream world of our own creation? So in this sense, is the premise of the movie, *The Matrix*, really only a work of science fiction?

As hard as it may seem at first, our ability to focus and concentrate can certainly be *practiced*, and our progress in perfecting such a skill would most definitely be worthwhile. It is not our ability to think that makes us human. Rather, it is our conscientious ability to correct and adjust ourselves that is truly unique to the human realm. To live is merely to exist. But to err and to improve ourselves is to be human. If we do not try to live in this way, then we give up that part of us that is human, as symbolized by the penalty of the Fellow Craft degree.

Those who may find the practice of calming down the mind to be difficult may say, "my brain is just wired this way" or "it is just human for me not to be able to quiet down my mind." But the latest research in neuroscience is proving otherwise! The entire field of *neuroplasticity* has opened, where science has proven that our thoughts and our experiences can actually shape the physical qualities of our brains – not simply the other way around. The millennia-old "mind-body problem" of Western philosophy may be slowly in the process of being addressed by this latest advancement in science. The brain does not just affect our thoughts. Our thoughts can actually affect the physical structure of the brain itself. So which comes first? The mind or the material? Well, don't answer that question. If we try to, then we neglect what we learned as Entered Apprentices – that Truth and reality exist beyond dualities! Chicken-or-the-egg questions and the mind-body problem are paradoxes only because we think of all things as existing as separate entities, when in fact, they are merely two sides of the same coin. As we have learned, we need to leave behind the world of dualities. When we leave behind the duality of time – the past and the future – then we live in the present. As Eleanor Roosevelt put it:

Yesterday is history.
Tomorrow is mystery.
Today is a gift.
That's why we call it
"The present."

BEYOND KNOWLEDGE AND SENSES

As we climb the spiral staircase in the Fellow Craft degree, we are taught the importance of obtaining knowledge and of educating ourselves in the worldly arts and sciences. By understanding the facts about the world at large, we become more capable of conducting our lives in a way that maximizes our worth as human beings. By understanding the laws of nature, we have learned to build civilizations far surpassing the imaginations of those who walked this planet centuries or even decades ago. My grandmother, when she was a child, once wondered whether humans would ever be able to travel to the moon. To her pleasant surprise, her question was answered affirmatively during her lifetime thanks to the scientific advancements of astronomy and engineering. As Masons, we are taught the importance of geometry and of other arts and sciences that serve as the foundation upon which the civilized world is built.

Knowledge, such as astronomy, can be intimately tied to the virtue of humility, as the late Carl Sagan demonstrated in his words about a distant image of earth from the Voyager spacecraft:

We succeeded in taking that picture [from deep space], and, if you look at it, you see a dot. That's here. That's home. That's us. On it, everyone you ever heard of, every human being who ever lived, lived out their lives. The aggregate of all our joys and sufferings, thousands of confident religions, ideologies and economic doctrines, every hunter and forager, every hero and coward, every creator and destroyer of civilizations, every king and peasant, every young couple in love, every hopeful child, every mother and father, every inventor and explorer, every teacher of morals, every corrupt politician, every superstar, every supreme leader, every saint and sinner in the history of our species, lived there on a mote of dust, suspended in a sunbeam.

The earth is a very small stage in a vast cosmic arena. Think of the rivers of blood spilled by all those generals and emperors so that in glory and in triumph they could become the momentary masters of a fraction of a dot. Think of the endless cruelties visited by the inhabitants of one corner of the dot on scarcely distinguishable inhabitants of some other corner of the dot. How frequent their misunderstandings, how eager they are to kill one another, how fervent their hatreds. Our posturings, our imagined self-importance, the delusion that we have some privileged position in the universe, are challenged by this point of pale light.

Our planet is a lonely speck in the great enveloping cosmic dark. In our obscurity – in all this vastness – there is no hint that help will come from elsewhere to save us from ourselves. It is up to us. It's been said that astronomy is a humbling, and I might add, a character-building experience. To my mind, there is perhaps no better demonstration of the folly of human conceits than this distant image of our tiny world. To me, it underscores our responsibility to deal more kindly and compassionately with one another and to preserve and cherish that pale blue dot, the only home we've ever known.

Profound humility arises from our knowledge of our place in the universe. It liberates us from our selfish egos and the assertion that how *we* view the world is always correct. The knowledge we learn and the facts we obtain come from our five senses. The way we interpret the world starts by our senses of taste, touch, sight, sound, and smell. But is what we taste, touch, see, hear, and smell all there is to the world? Like wearing a pair of prescription glasses, which are different depending on the person, our senses observe the world through our own interpretations. These "lenses" filter the details, depending on our prescription – our thoughts, emotions, and feelings. Why do certain people interpret a piece of artwork differently than others? Aren't we living in the same world? Well physically, yes; but mentally, no.

Our interpretations of the world around us are entirely subjective. When we realize this, we naturally invigorate our spirit of humility, because we know that how we see the world may be different from that of our peers and our colleagues. So why rush to judgment about someone who disagrees with us? Why not acknowledge that we each have our own interpretations of the world around us? We do not and could not agree with everyone, but we can certainly respect people for who they are even if we disagree. We can stand on the level with them, particularly those who share our journey of life.

The orders of architecture described in the Fellow Craft degree symbolically teach us that there are different ways for us to walk our journey of self-realization, much like there are different ways to design a building. As long as we wish to journey from darkness to light, there are no specifications as to exactly how we should walk or in what direction. It is up to us to discover for ourselves. This is also embodied in the Masonic principle of freedom of religion. Like crossing a river, if our goal is to reach the other shore, there can be many different ways to cross. Some may want to swim, others may want to canoe, and still others may want to build a raft. Some methods are quicker than others, whereas some may more easily lead us astray in the strong currents of egoism and emotional temptation. Each has its pros and cons. But since we each have to walk our own journeys and have the responsibility to ford the river of life in our own ways, how do we have time to judge each other?

Let's build our own rafts while helping others build theirs. This is the ideal of religious tolerance. We do not need to follow all religions or claim that they are all equal. But we can respect each other as we try to figure out how to cross the river. Look at ourselves instead of pointing fingers. To cause any strife or anger in others while we promote our own religious ideologies is to succumb to the strong current of egoism and to take a major step backward in our own progress toward the other shore.

As we continue our climb, let's keep in mind that although knowledge is useful, it is still not our final

destination. Our climb is leading us to the middle chamber
of our minds. We are traveling inward. Our journey is that
from darkness to light. Let's remember that. While worldly
knowledge and scientific and technological advancements
can be great things, they can also do a lot of harm. From
human medical testing in the 20th century to the
proliferation of weapons of mass destruction, scientific
knowledge can easily magnify rather than alleviate human
suffering. There must be more to "light" than worldly
knowledge. If "darkness" symbolizes ignorance, then
"light" must symbolize wisdom.

Knowledge is the understanding of facts that can
be studied, whereas wisdom must be learned through
experience and contemplation. Knowledge is learned in
school. Wisdom is gained through life. Knowledge is
knowing something. Wisdom is putting it to practice. As
Brother Benjamin Franklin said somewhat facetiously:

*All mankind is divided into three classes: those that are immovable,
those that are movable, and those that move.*

It is only through critical analysis and questioning
in all aspects of our daily lives do we gain wisdom: wisdom
to deal with challenges, wisdom to learn from our mistakes,
wisdom to acknowledge and confront our faults, and
wisdom to surpass them. Bad people can be
knowledgeable. In fact, the worst criminals are usually the
ones who are most intelligent, but the wise are always
good. Accepting the challenges that come our way, rather
than refuting or making excuses, is an act of wisdom. In
the words of Brother Voltaire:

*Each player must accept the cards life deals him or her: but once they
are in hand, he or she alone must decide how to play the cards in order
to win the game.*

This is the power of wisdom. Knowledge is necessary and beneficial for the advancement of society. But, as we continue to seek such knowledge, we must never lose sight of what it means to be wise – to be a fellow human being whom all can look to and say, "We are in this together." And when we stumble, we must continue on, for life is but a movie. With each passing frame, the glory of the animation is realized only through the intangible concept of change: learning from the past, focusing on the moment, and preparing for the future. Without these elements, we become nothing but a motionless memory – cold, still, and lifeless. As we seek knowledge and educate ourselves as Fellow Crafts, we begin to approach the search of wisdom that is implicated by the Master Mason degree, for wisdom is the true light at the end of our journey.

V

Impermanence

Looking back on our journey thus far, we have learned many important lessons. As Entered Apprentices, we acknowledged the state of our ignorance as human beings who are often limited in perspective. We have learned to let go of our conceptualizations by thinking outside of the cave and considering the perspectives of others. We have studied the nature of interdependence. We have pondered the purpose of our journey. We have learned about our habitual tendencies to divide everything in life into artificial categories of black and white. As Fellow Crafts, we have learned to transcend those dualities and to see life as it *is*, rather than what we *think* it is. Through the pillars, we have come to understand the need for balance in life, devoid of extremes. Through the symbolism of climbing the spiral staircase, we have learned the importance of living in the present moment and improving our lives by practicing mental focus and concentration. Now, as we enter the next phase of our journey as Master Masons, we begin to dig even deeper, where we must confront our biggest of enemies – our egos. Why is the ego our biggest foe? How can it prevent us from attaining lasting happiness?

Before we can address the issue of ego, we must first understand the concept of *change*. While mentioned briefly during our time as Entered Apprentices, we now consider it in more detail. In no uncertain terms, the Master Mason degree calls our attention to the inevitability of change in our lives. Through numerous symbols and allegories, the degree challenges us to face the truth of *impermanence*. As much as we try to ignore the fact that nothing is permanent, we cannot escape it. We can bring our cars into the shop for extra tune-ups each year, we can apply makeup when our skin starts to wrinkle, we can try to keep the floodwaters at bay by installing levees, but alas, when it is time for change to occur, it does so mercilessly.

It is easy to acknowledge change in our daily lives with respect to the external world. We are all aware of the change in seasons and the gradual breakdown of our material possessions. On the more human side, we are quick to note any changes in the physical appearances or personalities of longtime acquaintances. Perhaps a friend returns from vacation and we say, "Looks like you got quite a tan!" We usually cannot help but notice the new haircut that a colleague obtained over the weekend. Or we are quick to point out when a friend or associate changes his or her mind about something that was promised. "I thought you said you would never do something like this? You've changed," we assert.

Change may be hardly noticeable on a day-to-day basis, but over time, it is undeniable. Like an hourglass, the constant flow of the tiny grains of sand is difficult to observe. The amount of sand in either the upper or lower portions of the hourglass do not seem to change much as we watch. But, if we leave for a few minutes – or briefly doze off in a daydream – and then return to the hourglass, we are astonished at the amount of change that has occurred in that short amount of time. "Wow, that week went by fast!" we exclaim. And yet, as we continue to think about the past or dream about the future and totally neglect the beauty and value of each passing sand grain, we miss the true experience of life. Someone who remains fully aware, alert, and productive for seven days probably will not look back and say that the week passed quickly in vain.

In that hourglass, the miracle of time is manifested in the motion of those tiny, individual sand grains. Without that motion, we see no evidence of time. We do not need to be physicists in order to understand the implication of Einstein's Theory of Relativity: that space and time are inseparable. If the sand in an hourglass were not moving, would we be able to tell time? On the other hand, without the passage of time, would we be able to see the movement of the sand in an hourglass? Time is merely our observation of changes in space. And space is the product of changes in time. Space depends on time. Time depends on space. Without one, there cannot be the other – another example of non-duality.

While it is relatively easy to notice change in our external world, it is much more difficult for us to acknowledge change within ourselves. In fact, our peers may notice changes in our minds and personalities well before we do. This is partially a byproduct of our egos' inability to accept change. We subconsciously refuse to acknowledge our own place in the flow of time. We cling to our existence of an unchanging *self* so strongly, that when our peers observe and tell us that we have changed in a certain way, we may quickly fire back defensively. So it has become taboo in modern society to make any comment about how someone has changed over time. Likewise, for someone who has left the years of youth behind, saying something like, "Wow, you haven't changed one bit!" has become a standard compliment.

Why has society and human culture in general become so deeply rooted in the fear of change? By avoiding or covering up the appearance of change, do we alter or abolish the reality of impermanence? Or are we ultimately fooling ourselves by postponing our realization of the inevitable? The Master Mason degree encourages us to ponder these questions. By embracing change, we can more easily transcend the fearful barrier that keeps us from cherishing what we have. As a result, we can live life to the fullest, each and every waking moment.

Remember now thy Creator in the days of thy youth, while the evil days come not. Nor the years draw nigh when thou shalt say, I have no pleasure in them; While the sun, or the light, or the moon, or the stars, be not darkened, nor the clouds return after the rain. In the day when the keepers of the house shall tremble, and the strong men shall bow themselves, and the grinders cease because they are few, and those that look out of the windows be darkened. And the doors shall be shut in the streets, when the sound of the grinding is low, and he shall rise up at the voice of the bird, and all the daughters of music shall be brought low; Also, when they shall be afraid of that which is high, and fears shall be in the way. And the almond tree shall flourish and the grasshopper shall be a burden, and desire shall fail; Because man goeth to his long home, and the mourners go about the streets: Or ever the silver cord be loosed, or the golden bowl be broken, or the pitcher be broken at the fountain, or the wheel broken at the cistern. Then shall the dust return to the earth as it was; and the spirit shall return unto God who gave it.

This disconcerting passage, from Ecclesiastes 12: 1-7, is etched into the minds of all Master Masons – for good reason. It is an embodiment of the concept of *impermanence*, stating that while we all experience a phase of youth and vigor, that vitality must sooner or later pass. As the hourglass runs, energy and vigor give way to old age, frailty, and death. It is a fact of life that is inescapable. While the sun, the moon, and the stars continue to shine, the keeper of our physical bodies must sooner or later tremble at the thought of what lies ahead. Even the strong must bow down to the inevitable. Our teeth lose their ability to grind.

Our eyes lose their ability to discern. We wake at the slightest cry of the bird. Our voices become low and hoarse. The hair on our heads whitens, like a tree with almond-colored leaves. We lose our strength, so even a grasshopper seems heavy. Our many desires fade, seeing the futility of fighting the oncoming wave of change that will return us to our long home. While our loved ones may line the streets in mourning, we must still go. Our bodies break, piece by piece, slowly but surely, until finally, they are reduced to the dust from which they came, only to give up that part of us that abides in the Truth and the light of who we really are. So ends the story of our visible manifestations here on earth. Returning to the question we asked ourselves as Entered Apprentices, do we even "own" our physical bodies?

Some have described this passage in the Holy Bible as creepy, haunting, or even depressing. But how is an accurate description of our inevitable human fate at all depressing? Should it not be uplifting to know that we can have the strength *now* to accept what is to come and live life accordingly? Like the actions of a scythe on a field of wheat, the actions of time tear down all people and all things. Neither the tallest mountain, nor the largest ocean, nor the most powerful potentate can withstand the wrath of time. We all must drop to our knees in the face of *impermanence*. But this can and should be uplifting.

As we learned in the Fellow Craft degree, we must ever remember, "…that we are traveling upon the Level of Time to 'that undiscovered country, from whose bourne no traveler returns.'" Indeed, *impermanence* is our ultimate form of equality on the Level of Time. It is the greatest reality check. No matter how rich, how strong, or how fortunate we are, anything and everything we possess – including our physical bodies – must follow the winds of change. Likewise, no matter how poor, how weak, or how unfortunate we are, those things will pass *with time*. Therefore, when praises and fortunes are heaped on us, we should remain humble. When sorrow and misfortunes bury us, we should remain hopeful. All things pass, the good and the bad. That is the nature of life. Refusing to accept change is what brings much of our emotional strife. This was beautifully illustrated in the dialogue between Master Yoda and Jedi Anakin Skywalker in *Star Wars: Episode III – Revenge of the Sith (2005)*:

YODA: Premonitions...premonitions...Hmmmm...these visions you have...

ANAKIN: They are of pain, suffering, death...

YODA: Yourself you speak of, or someone you know?

ANAKIN: Someone...

YODA: ...close to you?

ANAKIN: Yes.

YODA: Careful you must be when sensing the future, Anakin. The fear of loss is a path to the dark side.

ANAKIN: I won't let these visions come true, Master Yoda.

YODA: Death is a natural part of life. Rejoice for those around you who transform into the Force. Mourn them, do not. Miss them, do not. Attachment leads to jealousy. The shadow of greed, that is.

ANAKIN: What must I do, Master Yoda?

YODA: Train yourself to let go of everything you fear to lose.

Chapter V

While it may be easy to dismiss this dialogue as nothing more than a scene from a movie, we should ponder the philosophical teaching that is contained. Herein lies the most deep-seated problem in human life – our struggle against the forces of change. What happened during the rest of this episode of *Star Wars*? In an attempt to do everything he could to save his wife from inevitable death, Anakin joined "The Dark Side." He surrendered to the very thing that he had devoted his life to fighting against. This "Dark Side" can be symbolically related to our daily lives as ignorance, hatred, envy, greed, and all the negative passions of man. There is absolutely nothing wrong with mourning or missing the loved ones we have lost. That is only human. It is not the emotions that are bad. Rather, our suffering comes from our incessant *attachment* to wanting control of something over which we have no control. Thus, we must train ourselves to let go of everything we fear to lose – especially once they are lost.

This "training" does not devalue anything. Instead, we learn to cherish every moment we have with our loved ones, so that once the sand in their hourglasses runs out, we can continue on our journey toward light and help others *help themselves* do the same, before we too need to enter that "undiscovered country." Do we really have time for petty arguments with our loved ones?

Understanding and accepting that our physical lives are finite is not depressing. It is also not a form of nihilism. It is only nihilism if we think that because we are coming to an end, we can do whatever we want right now and splurge on resources and physical pleasures. Such a thought only arises if we believe that there is nothing more beyond death. Science cannot prove life after death. So many people choose to believe that nothing exists after our physical bodies die. Yet that notion is also just a belief. Science cannot prove life after death, but it also cannot

78

prove that life *does not* exist after death. That is an important, logical breakdown that many of us overlook. While life after death has generally been assigned to the domain of faith and religion, we can do much to address this major question by understanding our current life *experiences* within the context of religion-neutral Masonic philosophy. But first, we must confront our egos and dig deeper to find out who we really are underneath the waves of change.

THE FALSE EGO

Recall that in Plato's story, the men in the cave are attached to their chairs by chains that keep them from moving or even turning their heads. What is a good analogy for these chains? What part of us is bitterly attached to what we *think* we know, thereby keeping us from seeing what is beyond our limited, personal perspectives? What part of us is offended when others disagree with us? Our egos.

Western developmental psychology frequently emphasizes the need for a healthy ego or a strong self-esteem in order for a child to grow into responsible, confident adults. While confidence and fortitude are good side effects of a "healthy" ego, more often than not, confidence can quickly transition to pride and conceit if the ego is not controlled. But rather than controlling our egos, why not consider the alternative of simply understanding what it is? When we *understand* the reality behind the shadow of ego, the negative side effects will naturally subside. So far on our journey toward light, a useful tactic to confront our challenges has always been to understand the *true nature* of the issue at hand. Otherwise, we will always be trapped by dualistic questions such as how much ego is good and how much is bad. Rather than thinking of ego as being "healthy" or "unhealthy," let's simply try to understand what it really is.

When asked, "Who are you?" How would we normally answer? We may first describe our names, where we're from, our nationalities, or even our family backgrounds. Digging deeper, we perhaps describe our interests, hobbies, ambitions, personalities, and emotional tendencies. But are any of these concrete? Do we have a certain set of characteristic traits that *never* change with time? When we say that we are athletic, what happens when we get old and can no longer play sports as well as we used to? When we say that we are faithful, what happens when that faith is tested by a string of extremely unfortunate circumstances? When we say that we are compassionate, what happens when our help with charity is unappreciated? When we say that we are smart or have a good memory, who are we when we get Alzheimer's? Conversely, negative traits can also change for the good. When someone says that we are selfish, who do we become when a photo of a starving child inspires us to contribute to humanitarian relief? When someone says that we are overweight, what happens when we hold fast to a rigorous workout program and transform ourselves into physically fit individuals? When someone says that we are shy, who do we become when we practice and master the art of public speaking?

We would be hard-pressed to find any characteristic, trait, interest, emotion, or adjective that can describe who we *always* are. Even the mental realm cannot escape the scythe of time because of the natural law of change that is brought about by causes, conditions, and effects. When an apple tree requires nutrients, water, sunlight, and air in order to survive and grow, the removal of any one of those conditions will kill the tree. If a tree is *dependent* upon a unique combination of causes and conditions in order to exist, and if those causes and conditions individually change with time, then isn't it only natural for the existence of the tree to be limited in time? When the conditions change, so does the tree. The same goes for the physical and non-physical aspects of human life. Since our self-identities, or egos, are dependent upon a set of descriptors, once any of those characteristics change, then the concept of *self* necessarily changes as well. Thus, the *self* is an intangible concept that evades description. But because we choose to believe otherwise, and oftentimes get offended when someone "injures" our own notion of who we are, the illusion that we possess an unchanging self-identity can be deemed the *false ego*.

The fact that no words can describe who we are is neither a belief nor a religious assertion. It is a conclusion that we can draw based on our own *experiences*. As with everything we have learned on our journey, there is always a benefit to applying a particular philosophy to our daily lives. By doing so, we make it a part of us. How is the concept of false ego beneficial? When we dissolve our sense of a concrete, never-changing self-identity, we liberate our minds from the tendencies toward bias, prejudice, and conceit. By believing that we are a certain set of adjectives, we cling to the illusion that we are always a certain way. Thus, when others perceive us a different way, we can easily get insulted or offended. Furthermore, we limit ourselves when we think that we cannot change. The source of existential angst or depression can often be traced back to a person's belief that he was born with a particular fault or weakness that cannot be changed. He may *believe* that nothing can be done to change his predicament. But that is just a *belief*! Why cling to an illusion? If there exists something that is impossible to change, then the law of impermanence would break down.

But through logical analysis and critical thinking, we see that in the world of conditioned phenomena, there are no counterexamples to the law of impermanence. So goes the saying that the only thing certain in life is that nothing is certain.

By realizing that we do not possess an intrinsic, never-changing self-identity and that we are not fixed to a particular set of adjectives, we liberate ourselves to an infinite realm of possibilities. By being nothing in particular, we can be anything! A blank sheet of paper is the most valuable possession of an illustrator, because it can transform into an infinite number of possible scenes. Our potential for success and happiness are boundless. They only depend on our mindsets. Furthermore, when we realize that we have no fixed, describable identity, who can possibly insult us? The next time someone wrongly criticizes us for something that we know we aren't, we can respond with emotional pragmatism. Like a raindrop that rolls off the sleeve of a GORE-TEX® jacket, why let any insult cling to us? We can never control what happens to us, but we can always control how we respond to each situation. By thinking in this way, our negative emotions naturally cease, and we remain at peace, like a sturdy building that stands strong as the storms pass by. In this way, we build our self-confidence without the negative side effects of egoism.

Who are we underneath the false ego? What do we truly *own* underneath our false egos? For the sake of aiding in communication, philosophers and religious leaders have often used the term "soul" to describe that part of us that continues past the physical realm. However, the use of that word can often be misleading. It can imply that there is an inherently unchanging self-identity that persists, but that is not the true meaning behind the term "soul."

By saying that there is no inherently unchanging self-identity, we are *not* saying that there is *nothing* that persists beyond the physical realm. Based on sound logic, just because we determine that a concept is *not* true does not necessarily mean that the opposite *is* true! To think that way would be to fall once again under the influence of dualistic thought. Just because something is not white does not imply that it is black. To think that way would be to neglect the entire spectrum of colors.

The concept of false ego is not an existential issue. We are not saying whether we truly exist or do not exist. A more proper analogy for the false ego would be like the common misunderstanding we have of waves on the ocean. What is a wave? From the macroscopic view, a wave appears to be an identifiable *object* that moves and transports water and surfers across the surface of the ocean. But in reality, a wave is nothing more than water parcels moving up and down with minimal horizontal displacement. A wave propagates. It does not actually transport any water. A log that floats on the surface of the ocean will only bob up and down when a wave passes underneath. It will not be carried with the wave. Surfers only travel across the surface of the water because they are riding the front side of the wave and making use of gravity and the buoyancy of water to accelerate them. In reality, the wave does not transport any mass with it. Only the energy propagates. Much like tying a slinky to the wall and swinging it until it forms a wave that travels back and forth across the room, the slinky as a whole does not move toward or away from the wall.

So what is the reality of a wave? Is it not just part of the ocean that manifests *temporarily* due to certain causes and conditions? Thus, the appearance of the wave as a separately existing, traveling entity that is distinct from the ocean is merely an *illusion*, much like our concept of an unchanging self-identity.

THE THREE CHALLENGES

In the process of becoming a Master Mason, we must confront three primary challenges. Each challenge meets us by surprise, forcing us to dive into the depths of our minds to consider the meanings of fortitude and honor. As a whole, they symbolize our enemies from within – our loss of the mastership of our own minds due to our insatiable desires, uncontrollable emotions, and ceaseless vexations. More specifically, the challenges can be described as a chronological summary of the hurdles that we all face in life.

The first challenge comes from our own evil passions, bad habits, and negative thoughts that cause strife to others and to ourselves. Our greed, hatred, anger, licentiousness, ignorance – all these states of mind, while difficult to unravel, can eventually be overcome. Through our diligent *practice* of Freemasonry and the application of its philosophies to our daily lives, we slowly mold the rough ashlars of our minds into that which is fit to build our most sturdy, spiritual edifices. We gradually become better people and make wise use of our limited time here on earth. But, even as we perfect ourselves, we are met with another challenge.

The second hurdle that we confront in life comes from the events we cannot control. We must confront the pain of illness, financial distress, misfortune, and other adversaries. Many of these events may seem unfair to someone who has been diligently molding his rough ashlar, but the purpose of this second hurdle is to test his resolve. Although we may be doing the right things, do we truly possess the fortitude to continue in the face of brutal challenges that occur to us later in life? Or, will we succumb to emotional whims and fall into moral turpitude?

For those who may overcome even the second hurdle, the last and most difficult challenge is that of accepting *impermanence*. No matter how strong, how beautiful, or how successful a person, the hourglass has the final word. While we may be able to confront the first and second hurdles in life, there is no escape from the third. Instead, we must learn to *live* with it. Whether we are met with the loss of a loved one or are confronted by our own inevitable destiny, we must learn to understand and cope with the reality of impermanence. It is up to us to decide how we want to view this reality. We can ignore it, cover it up, or let it tear us down in depression and futility. Or, if we are wise, we will let it inspire us to value each moment and each day of life as a rare gift to be cherished and used wisely.

Looking at the big picture, what is the purpose of these three hurdles in life? They serve to *eradicate our false egos*. They tear our false sense of pride down, one step at a time, one blow at a time. But as we persevere, we realize the importance of circumscribing our passions. We begin to see that part of us that lies underneath the transience of characteristics. Adversity is often necessary for our spiritual progress in life. Without it, we do not see our faults, and we do not know where we need to improve.

Not being able to look past our false egos lies beneath the symbolism of the penalty of the Master Mason degree. We can only be raised after our false egos are dissolved. With this comes a genuine sense of compassion, which arises when we see that through interdependence, beneath our varying characteristics, emotions, thoughts, and interests, we all truly stand on the level. Underneath all the colors, shapes, and textures, every type of artwork is painted onto blank canvases that are equal. The final scenes are different, but the fundamental canvases are the same. Understanding the impermanence of self-identity frees us from the shackles of greed that come from feeding our false egos. We then become the masters of our emotions, rather than being enslaved by them. The true Master Mason is the master of himself.

RIVERS OF LIFE

If someone were to show you a series of photographs taken of you at various stages of your life, which one would you select to represent you? If one were randomly chosen, would it represent you any more than the others? If not, then how can the first question be answered? What is the source of this paradox? Clearly, the issue of *change* implies the breakdown of any attempt to describe the continuity of life. Rather than reconciling the apparent paradox between change and continuity, let's make use of another symbol to help us better understand who we are.

Much wisdom lies in the river as a symbol for human life. A river is a product of causes and conditions. As a flowing entity, it embodies the essence of change. It manifests in different forms and defies control. It meanders through changing terrain, sometimes rocky, other times smooth. It resists nothing, always going with the flow. But, it is steadfast, cutting a path whenever it is necessary. It is soft, yet strong. It can be slow, yet it can be a raging rapid. It transcends dualities and eludes description.

The Greek philosopher Heraclitus once said:

You cannot step twice into the same river.

With nothing but one symbol in one sentence, the law of impermanence was captured millennia ago. It is now up to us to apply this wisdom to our own lives. A river is a constantly flowing body of water. It never ceases to be in motion. The moment we apply a description to it, the river has changed and the description becomes invalid. No two ripples on the surface of the water are exactly the same, so the appearance of a river as a fixed entity on a map is nothing but an illusion. Thus, we cannot step into the same river twice. Indeed, we can go so far as to say that we cannot even step into the same river *once*!

The illusion that a river can be accurately described or will always remain in its same state is much like the notion of the false ego. Attempting to assign adjectives to ourselves is much like measuring the length, width, depth, and flow rate of a river, completely overlooking the fact that it changes, from moment to moment, depending on the weather, geography, and other environmental *conditions*. People are like rivers, ever changing, but appearing fixed, coming together for a while and then drifting away. The people we meet along our winding journey, including our friends and loved ones, are like neighboring rivers that come into our lives for a while, then departing, most often not a product of our control. When it is time to go, it is time to go. So why despair at our parting of ways? Instead, let us rejoice in the time we can spend together and focus on making a positive impact in the flow of that neighboring river, for that is our legacy.

We must go with the flow, but have a destination in mind. Like water, we must be strong, capable of cutting a path through the sturdiest of rock; but also flexible, capable of filling any container of any shape. Rivers transcend the dualities of permanence and transience, power and obedience. So it is with us. We are but rivers, flowing constantly in the flux of change, from raging cascades to trickling flows; meandering through life's twists and turns, never satisfying our expectations of the scene just around the next bend; but ever cherishing those miles that we can flow together with other beloved rivers at our sides, for at last, even the mightiest of rivers must part and continue their own journeys. The next time we come across a river on our trail, let's pause for a moment of reflection...

Who am I?

VI

The Lost Traveler

When asked what he has come to lodge to do, the Entered Apprentice responds with his task to reign in his passions and emotions. These, together with the symbol of the square and compasses, form the core of what it means to be a Mason. We have discussed the importance of these ideals throughout our journey, but let us take a few moments to elucidate *how* we should properly go about the task. This will lead us to see what lies *underneath* our false egos, wherein the true prize of a Master Mason can be found.

By definition, Truth cannot contradict reason, yet prudence and rational thought are often compromised by strong emotions. This is not to say that emotions are *bad*. By now, such an absolute statement should not even cross our minds, since we have transcended the world of dualities. Clearly, to be human is to have feelings and emotions. But with this in mind, how do we carry out the primary task of being a Mason?

A past master of Norman Lodge No. 38 once said to me prior to my initiation, "We habitually grab on to a passing train, not knowing to what station we are headed. We have to learn to *let go* of the train and watch as it passes." This cryptic statement actually bore great meaning, as I had come to learn over the years. The train is our thoughts, our emotions, and our feelings. It represents the integrated portion of the consciousness that gives rise to our ignorant self-identities and false egos. When left completely unchecked, our emotional rollercoaster ride leaves us constantly uncertain and unsatisfied with life. Worse, we may act in ways that bring us regret in the future. To be more fully in tune with our lives, we must learn to properly deal with our passions and emotions. We must see them for what they are. Like the changing weather, we must acknowledge their presence, but let them go as they pass with time.

Learning to let go of our emotions is not to deny or suppress them. Their existence is not the problem. Rather, it is our habitual *clinging* to our emotions that often brings unwanted consequences. When someone cuts us off on the highway, frustration and anger immediately well up within us. We yell, scream, and honk our horns. This angers the driver ahead of us, who then slams on his breaks. We curse, yell some more, and give the middle finger. The driver stops and gets out of his car... Does the story end here? You can fill in the blanks.

Road rage is a common example of our passions spiraling out of control. What begins as a relatively benign and innocent mistake can quickly magnify into a full-scale conflict if we *cling* to our emotions. We dig ourselves a deeper hole or may do something we regret later. Our initial frustration directed at the driver who cut us off was a habitual response to something that infringed on our expectations. While this initial response was a reflection of instinctive human emotion, what happens afterward is our responsibility. Do we let it go? Or do we act and *cling* to that emotion until it amplifies beyond our control? Like dribbling a basketball, the harder we hit it, the higher it will bounce.

Anger is the most inflammatory human emotion. It renders our minds incapable of functioning normally. Rational thought and logic take a backseat when we are angry, and we become drunk off of that burning sensation within our chests. Many people have the innate ability to quell their anger after some time, while others may easily lose control of themselves. To lose ourselves is to give up our free will to our emotions and to let them control us. In effect, we regress in our journey toward light. We give up temperance and prudence for the sake of retribution, even at our own expense. Anger is like reaching into a box of loose knives in order to grab one to throw at someone. We are the ones who would get cut first.

Do we solve anything by cursing and throwing expletives at the driver ahead of us? Could he even hear us? And if he could, do we really think he would simply bow down in apology and stroke our egos? Why not save our own energy and reduce the stress of our passengers. There is never a reason to cling to anger. Our mental energy can always be directed at more useful tasks, like directly solving the problem at hand, or moving on. Some may say that anger can be beneficial when it is directed at promoting a good cause. While strong emotion can serve as a catalyst for action, a person who is truly fighting for what is right exhibits great fortitude and resolve, not anger.

Freemasonry constantly reminds us to approach our emotions with pragmatism and restraint. But in order to succeed, we must understand the difference between restraint and suppression. When we attempt to suppress our emotions, such an unnatural state of mind may only generate further vexations. Modern psychology would agree that suppressing our inner tendencies and emotions, including anger, would be like placing a lid over a simmering pot of water. An explosion may someday result. So rather than suppressing or stopping our emotions, we should simply learn to *let go* of them as they pass. By *disassociating* ourselves from our emotions, rather than identifying with them, we succeed in restraining our passions without having to suppress or forcibly control them.

Instead of grabbing onto a train as it speeds by, take a few moments to *watch* it carefully as it passes. See it. Acknowledge it. Pay attention to it. Notice the shapes, the colors, and the details. We often grab on to our emotions without even knowing what they are. We've all had sluggish days when we remain in a perpetual bad mood – without even knowing why. We just call it a "bad day," or we blame the uncontrollable circumstances around us for how we feel. But who is ultimately responsible for our emotions? Who can we truly blame outside of ourselves for what goes on in our own minds? By analyzing our thoughts and emotions, we understand ourselves better. By paying attention to the structure of the train, we become more aware of each moment in our lives. Not doing so results in confusion, and we may end up in an unfamiliar situation – or train station – against our good judgment.

The key is to *let go* of the train, *not* to try and stop it. Emotions are not problematic. The train is not the source of our problems. Rather, it is our habitual clinging to something we don't fully understand that ultimately leads us astray. If we were to try and suppress our emotions, it would be like standing in front of the train to stop it. We would be swiftly run over. Avoiding the extremes of attachment and suppression will keep us on the right track, and even a bad day at work becomes easier to handle.

Although we used negative emotions as examples in our train analogy, the concept of emotional restraint should also apply to seemingly good emotions. This is because too much of anything will bring unwanted consequences, as the two pillars taught us. But some may wonder, "If we don't cling to the train and ride the roller coaster of emotions, then wouldn't life be boring?" We must not fall back into the duality of the checkered pavement. To say that we should avoid something does not necessarily imply the existence of the opposite. Detaching ourselves from our emotional trains is *not* to say that we become emotionless, boring, or inhuman. We still watch the trains go by. We still acknowledge them. They still exist. But we see them for what they are. We see them as temporary, passing phenomena like everything else in the world. In effect, we do not trap or fool ourselves by the illusion of something that may eventually spiral out of control. Anger, like any other emotion, comes and goes, so why let it consume us? This practice of detachment, instead of leading us to boredom, allows us to go anywhere and be in any circumstance while maintaining a level of inner peace. This inner tranquility transforms into a steady, blissful contentment that persists far beyond those that any temporary, sensory pleasures can maintain.

A person may have offended us fifteen years ago with something that they did. But if we continuously think and remind ourselves of that event and have a hint of anger grow within us each time we remember that incident, then are we not repeating the offense with our own will? Someone may have stabbed us once. But we stab ourselves hundreds of times by *clinging* to emotions of the past. We would be a fool not to let go of what has passed. In this manner, forgiveness is truly a virtue. It is not only a moral or religious issue, but also a pragmatic one that we should embrace for our own benefit.

The careful analysis of how we should approach the issue of emotional pragmatism is one of the greatest tasks of the Master Mason. While the notion of restraining our passions and emotions was introduced to us as Entered Apprentices and has been a recurring theme in all the degrees, the Master Mason degree reinforces the importance of paying attention to our thoughts. The Tyler's Sword teaches us to guard our thoughts with vigilance and circumspection, as the Tyler guards the door of his lodge. The reason for this can be found in the following quote from Mahatma Gandhi:

Keep your thoughts positive, because your thoughts become your words. Keep your words positive, because your words become your behaviors. Keep your behaviors positive, because your behaviors become your habits. Keep your habits positive, because your habits become your values. Keep your values positive, because your values become your destiny.

If our thoughts, emotions, feelings, biases, and judgments come and go and are ever changing with time, then what more is there to who we are? If nothing is permanent, then what is the part of us that transcends the temporary? What lies underneath the ephemeral? Is there any part of us that is continuous, regardless of the changes that govern the material world? If there is, how do we *experience* or logically understand that part of us without surrendering to blind faith? How can these philosophical inquiries be applied as practical tools that help us in our daily lives? These questions, my brother, form the ultimate core of our mission as Master Masons. They require our constant attention. They comprise the *unfinished* work that awaits us in the sanctum sanctorum of our minds.

THE LOST WORD

"Remember now thy Creator in the days of thy youth…" Remember *now* thy Creator – not tomorrow, not later, not after we finish this television show – but *now*. Regardless of what religions we follow, we are called forth to seek our original source – our *true nature*. We must accept this task immediately, in the present moment, in our youth, because we do not know what challenges may lie ahead. But we can do so without suspending the other obligations in our lives. We can ponder the deepest questions of life and seek our *true nature* while eating, working, driving, or sitting in lodge. This is because our *true nature* is always with us. It is right here. There is no escaping it. What we are looking for – what has been lost – has always been present. But, it lies dormant, underneath our fleeting thoughts, emotions, and feelings – overshadowed by our ignorance. It is buried underneath our false egos. Who we truly are serves as the foundation of all that we *think* we are. It is that beautiful, white canvas underneath all the colors of a masterpiece. It is the clear water that has always been a part of the mud. It is that light outside the cave that has always been there. We just need to be enlightened to its presence.

An overriding theme of the Master Mason degree is the search for a word that has been lost. This word is symbolic of the deepest secret of Freemasonry – the fundamental essence of man and his relationship with the universe. It embodies Absolute Truth and the ultimate climax of our journey. And yet, as hard as we look for it, we never find it. Instead, we must be satisfied with a substitute or replacement for the lost word, until someday, somewhere, we find the original word in all its glory. The enigma of the lost word should naturally be aggravating and unsatisfying to the newly made, inquisitive Master Mason. What is the purpose of this symbol? Why is the lost word so hard to find? How do we continue searching for something that has been lost for so long?

The substitute for the lost word teaches us that as men in the cave, no matter how hard we try to think or describe the light of day, we can never substitute words for the actual *experience* of light. Any concept or idea that is imposed on Absolute Truth must always fall short of describing the essence of reality. Like someone pointing to the sun, if we mistake the purpose and symbol of the finger for the actual object of the sun, then we are foolish. Likewise, if we believe that a concept, word, or book can substitute for the infinity of Truth, then we are but naives.

The symbol of the lost word was embodied in Western religious tradition by the words of St. John the Evangelist, "In the beginning was the Word, and the Word was with God, and the Word was God." By definition, in our ignorant state as humans living in the cave, we cannot fully comprehend the complete and spotless wisdom that coincides with the symbol of God or Absolute Truth, even if our egos *think* we can. Thus, our world is riddled with people who are so confident about their *version* of Truth that they go to great lengths to demean and degrade others for their different beliefs. They act as if their substitute for the lost word is the true one, and world conflicts throughout history have resulted from this delusion. This was illustrated by John Godfrey Saxe's poem in the nineteenth century, based on the ancient Indian parable, "The Blind Men and the Elephant:"

It was six men of Indostan
*   To learning much inclined,*
Who went to see the Elephant
*   (Though all of them were blind)*
That each by observation
*   Might satisfy the mind.*

The First approached the Elephant
*   And happening to fall*
Against his broad and sturdy side
*   At once began to bawl:*
"Bless me, it seems the Elephant
*   Is very like a wall!"*

The Second, feeling of his tusk,
   Cried, "Ho! What have we here
So very round and smooth and sharp?
   To me 'tis mighty clear
This wonder of an Elephant
   Is very like a spear!"

The Third approached the animal,
   And happening to take
The squirming trunk within his hands,
   Thus boldly up and spake:
"I see," quoth he, "the Elephant
   Is very like a snake!"

The Fourth reached out an eager hand,
   And felt about the knee.
"What most this wondrous beast is like
   Is mighty plain," quoth he;
"'Tis clear enough the Elephant
   Is very like a tree!"

The Fifth, who chanced to touch the ear,
   Said: "E'en the blindest man
Can tell what this resembles most;
   Deny the fact who can,
This marvel of an Elephant
   Is very like a fan!"

The Sixth no sooner had begun
   About the beast to grope,
Than, seizing on the swinging tail
   That fell within his scope,
"I see," quoth he, "the Elephant
   Is very like a rope!"

And so these men of Indostan
Disputed loud and long,
Each in his own opinion
Exceeding stiff and strong,
Though each was partly in the right
And all were in the wrong!

So oft in theologic wars,
The disputants, I ween,
Rail on in utter ignorance
Of what each other mean,
And prate about an Elephant
Not one of them has seen!

As human beings in our state of ignorance, we are like the men in the poem who attempt to describe the nature of the universe with only limited information, "though each was partly in the right and all were in the wrong." This poem teaches us that any description or personality that we impose upon God or Absolute Reality, symbolized by the elephant, will always be flawed and incomplete with respect to words and concepts. Truth cannot be described. It can only be experienced. This realization, that we are all partially blindfolded in our own ways, should augment our sense of humility when we cross paths with people whose beliefs differ from ours. This humility is the mark of a mature Master Mason. With it, we understand the necessity for religious tolerance, because until we are completely in unity with Truth, we cannot claim to understand its essence more than our fellow brothers and sisters. We can and should hold fast to our own beliefs, but we can do so while respecting others. Still, tolerating other religious ideas besides our own is only the first step. We must strive to stand *on the level* with our fellow human beings and transcend even the notion of tolerance.

We will have truly reached the perfection of tolerance when we realize that there is nothing to tolerate.

As we approach the sanctum sanctorum of our Masonic journey, the holy of holies of our mental abode, we must strive to finish the unfinished business of finding that which was lost. We must continue searching for that word, for it embodies the essence of humanity and establishes the reason for our existence. The act of seeking the word brings us closer to Truth. That is the purpose of our Masonic journey. Although some other Masonic organizations with additional degrees may profess to reveal the original word, that word is still only *symbolic* and not meant to permanently satisfy our quest to find the lost word. The purpose of the symbol of the lost word is to show that *no word* can be a suitable substitute for what it symbolizes. Yet, the closer we get to Truth, the closer we get to experiencing the lost word, and the clearer our view of life becomes. The search *is* the purpose of life. In the words of Brother J. Otis Ball:

It should be the purpose and the object of every true and worthy brother to find this Master's Word.

Although the legend of the Master Mason degree teaches the virtues of honor and fidelity, it contains a treasure trove of other deep, philosophical ideas that manifest upon closer inspection. Thinking back to the degree, who possessed the original word? With whom did it reside, and how was it lost? What was our role when it was lost? Deep and careful reflection on these questions lead us to realize that as a Master Mason and as a master of our own minds, to seek the Truth, we must look *inward*. We will never find it totally separate and distinct from the mind. It cannot be found in money. It does not reside in any of our material possessions.

Seeking and experiencing the essence of our true nature brings us closer to understanding the purpose of life and our place in the world. This message is echoed in all the major religious traditions of the world, with differences in syntax and nomenclature. Abrahamic religions teach that we were "created in the image of God," so we are a reflection of Truth. Likewise, some Eastern religions profess that the potential for understanding Truth rests in our ability to "wake up" or enlighten ourselves to the Truth within, because "inner Truth" and "universal Truth" are but two sides of the same coin. Both sentiments are similar, and in this sense, Freemasonry captures the essence of both Western and Eastern mysticism. The universality of introspection, contemplation, and self-awareness as a means to find the lost word cannot be overlooked.

Now, let us investigate the true nature that lies beneath our false egos and more fully realize its essence by returning to our analogy of the passing train. From the perspective of a person clinging to the side of a moving train, it is a vehicle that appears concrete and lasts indefinitely in our frame of view. That is much like a person who clings to his anger or depression. Doing so only perpetuates its existence. But once we succeed in letting go of our fleeting emotions, we become more *aware* of what they really are. From the perspective of an observer who stands still on the platform, the passing train is but a temporary phenomenon that comes and goes. From this absolute frame of reference, we no longer identify ourselves with something that is temporary. Instead, we notice that there is a part of us that does *not* depend on the things that change. We begin to see that in order for us to even *notice* our thoughts, feelings, and emotions, there must be an *observer* that is *separate* and *distinct* from them.

There must be something that is independent of our emotions, which allows us to be *aware* of them in the first place. We *know* when thoughts cross our minds. We *know* when we get angry. We *know* when our senses are activated. This "knowing" ability, our ability to *know* – this *awareness* of ours – is distinct from the thoughts themselves! When we feel hunger, we can identify that feeling. It is one that we assign to our stomachs. But is our *awareness* of the feeling of hunger *itself hungry*? When we get angry, does our *awareness* of that anger *itself* become angry? Indeed, the train and the person *watching* the train are two separate entities! So now, let's ask this question: If the observer of the passing train is *not* part of the train itself, then who is watching the train go by?

Our *awareness*, or our *ability to perceive*, defies description. It is a universal human ability. We all possess this *awareness*, regardless of our cultures or our educational backgrounds. It is not black or white, big or small, male or female, American or Asian. It is subtle, but ever present. When we describe someone's personality, we are describing the layers of consciousness *on top of* his awareness. Characteristics, emotions, thoughts, feelings, habits, biases, egos, likes, dislikes – all these things exist on top of the fundamental awareness that we all posses. All of these things are *conditioned* phenomena. Like a tree that depends on a set of conditions in order to exist, all elements of our consciousnesses depend on conditions that change with time. As the conditions change, so do they. That is why all adjectives that describe our thoughts and emotions change with time, like a passing train. However, the foundation of our consciousness, the blank canvas – our true nature – is that fundamental *awareness* that is always there. It cannot be described, but it is *there*.

We know that *awareness* is the fundamental state of the human mind because we must *perceive* something before any other element of consciousness can act. We must *see* a solid object in front of us before we can identify the object as a desk. We must *hear* a chirp before we can recognize the sound to be the call of a bird. We must *taste* sweetness and *feel* the carbonation before we can identify a beverage as soda. Our awareness must always *precede* our conceptualizations. First, we perceive something, then we conceptualize. Immediately afterward, we inject our judgments, biases, and preferences. These then lead to our desires and attachments. This chain of events happens so quickly that we usually do not notice its operation. But through this logical analysis, we have empirically proved to ourselves that our minds constantly operate on this sequence, moment by moment. By tracing this sequence back to the very beginning, we see that our *awareness* is the basic foundation of human consciousness.

When we cut through all the personalities that result from the layers of consciousness that distinguish us from other people, we confront an interesting realization. If the fundamental nature of life is this all-encompassing, indescribable *awareness* that evades conceptualization, then are we not travelers on equal footing in the face of Absolute Truth? Alas! We are all *fundamentally equal* at the core of our existence! Granted, we are not all equal when it comes to our unique talents, abilities, emotions, personalities, and actions; but these traits are all parts of the superficial layers of consciousness, which are obviously different depending on the person. But beneath all of these layers, our true nature and fundamental awareness stand together equally. My awareness – my ability to *know* – is not different from yours. We stand *on the level*, shoulder-to-shoulder, with our fellow brothers, mothers and fathers, sons and daughters, strangers and loved ones; not because of a political or ideological mandate, but because the fundamental essence of our being – beneath all the adjectives that describe our unique consciousnesses – is equal. Overlooking this fact of life would be to deny the inherent freedoms and universal rights possessed by each human being on earth. This misunderstanding has been the source of the greatest atrocities of mankind, from racism to genocide.

This description-less *awareness* parallels the theme of the lost word with respect to our inability to describe Absolute Truth with concepts. Even the term "awareness" is merely a substitute – a placeholder – for what it really is. To lose sight of our *awareness* would be to falsely associate our thoughts, feelings, and emotions with our true nature, which gives rise to our false egos. To break our false egos, to see ourselves for who we really are, and to see our fellow human beings as fundamentally equal creatures, is to find our true essence – the lost traveler.

While the discussion of our true nature of awareness may seem like nothing more than a philosophical exercise, there is actually an extremely useful application of this mental practice to our daily lives. Earlier, in our analogy of the train, we discussed the need to let go of our attachments to vexations by *watching* them pass, rather than suppress them, because that would be like standing in front of the train. The best way to stop a ball from bouncing is to let it go and just *watch* its oscillations dampen with time. Any attempt to hit it or suppress it will only force it to bounce higher. The same is true in our attempts to deal with anger. Rather than aggressively attacking ourselves by yelling, "No! Stop getting angry!" and directing the anger at ourselves each time we want to calm down, we should simply *let it go*. The best way to do so most effectively is to *focus on our awareness* of that anger.

To focus on our awareness – to abide in it – is to let go of the train and place our attention on the observer. Rather than the extremes of clinging to or suppressing our anger, we focus on that part of us that is *observing* it. We still acknowledge the presence of the anger, but by deflecting our attention to the observer, we dissociate ourselves from the emotion, and the power of the anger is diminished. In this manner, we guarantee that the anger will not carry us to some unknown territory that we regret later. It does not matter how much horsepower a train engine has. If I choose not to hold on to it, it cannot take me anywhere.

So try it! The next time you get angry, *notice* that exact moment when it arises. Focus on it. Take the "I'm angry" mentality and immediately convert it to, "Oh, I *see* that I'm angry...but who is really angry?" When you *see* and *focus* on the *awareness* of anger, rather than the anger itself, you immediately remove its power. Let go of the train and let it blow by. You are then liberated from its effects and can begin to solve your problem more effectively through rational and logical action.

We should put the symbolic wisdom of the lost word to practice on other mental vexations to free ourselves from their unwanted grip. Only then can true and lasting peace of mind be found. We can free ourselves from the effects of envy, greed, and hatred by abiding in our pure and spotless *awareness*, rather than clinging to or suppressing those emotions. Remember, there are never only two options.

Our true nature of awareness is that "emblem of innocence, and the badge of a Mason." Since we are admonished to keep it "pure and spotless," rather than covering it with the fleeting and the temporary, we should abide in it and live in its presence. In this way, instead of framing our actions merely in the context of "self control," we can more effectively address them in the context of "self awareness."

This is only one application of the practice of seeking the lost word in our daily lives. Can you think of others? What does it mean to you?

THE EVERGREEN SPRIG

The most profound aspect of the Master Mason degree is its unique combination of symbolism and drama, which brings to life the sobering reality of impermanence while carrying a resounding message of hope and inspiration. It teaches us that no matter how rich or poor, how famous or unknown, how beautiful or ugly we are, the playing field is leveled in the face of death. Our current life destinies begin with no more than a thought in our parents' minds. We are born. We grow up, educate ourselves about the world, then live our lives pursuing our dreams and aspirations. We ride the waves of hope and despair, wealth and destitution. Then, after just a brief time, our energy and vitality wane. We return to the earth, as the dust from which we once came. We travel to where our forefathers have gone before.

We are but a flash of lightning, passing through the pages of time in the blink of an eye. We live a perpetual dream, as a fragile bubble in the sky, an ephemeral ripple on the sea, and a speck of dust in the universe. But rather than let these realizations bring us down, we Master Masons learn that life is an adventure, waiting to be discovered down every path, under every boulder, across every river, atop every mountain. To the Master, the world is his trail; his mind, his treasure map. As brief and as small as our lives may seem in the grand scheme of the universe, we are only insignificant if we choose to be. In reality, each page in a book develops the story. Each episode in a television series motivates the plot. Each frame in a movie contributes to the animation.

As we ponder the inevitable destiny of our physical bodies, we are left to wonder, what happens afterward? Various religious traditions provide different ideas about the afterlife, and most of them require an element of faith that often depends on culture. While this is perfectly acceptable in the face of personal preferences and beliefs, is there anything in the Master Mason degree that can help us navigate the delicate balance of faith and experience with regard to the afterlife? The primary lesson and final task of the Master Mason is to seek the lost word, so let us return to our analysis of our *true nature*.

In our discussion of our awareness, we discovered that it cannot be described with concepts or words. It is simply *there*. Furthermore, any attempt to describe its function would be futile. But we know of its presence because we *experience* it and can prove its existence to ourselves each and every moment. As you read this page, you must first *see* and be *aware* of the ink on the paper before your conscious mind and memory identifies the words and assigns meanings to them. This identification process requires preexisting knowledge. Someone who cannot read English would not be able to assign meaning to the ink marks on this page. Likewise, if you cannot read Cyrillic, then the word осведомленности probably means nothing to you. Only a person who understands Russian would know that it says "awareness." However, our true nature does not depend on knowledge, because without it, knowledge could not be perceived. It underlies the changing elements of consciousness. Awareness always exists. Like the observer on the platform, trains can pass by, but he remains unmoved.

Contrary to our earlier discussion about conditioned phenomena, our awareness is *unconditioned*. Can you think of something that *caused* our awareness? Beyond our senses, which only affect the quality of our perception but not our *ability* to perceive, is there anything that precedes our capacity to *know* and to be *aware*? Can something that cannot be described have a cause? We cannot come up with a logical answer to this question. This is because, regardless of our changing mental and physical states, our true nature *transcends* even the concepts of change and time. Thus, nothing could *cause* it to exist. Something that is unconditioned means that it did not require a certain set of conditions to exist in the first place, so how can it ever die when other conditions change?

That which is unconditioned cannot perish! Like an evergreen tree, which is immune to the change of seasons, our true nature is unaffected by the physical realm. The leaves will always be green, no matter the circumstances. The evergreen sprig reminds us that our *awareness* will always be there, even during and after the deterioration of our physical bodies; it has been, and it always will be. There is no need to rely only on faith to understand this statement. Instead, let us contemplate this assertion using a few other simple thought problems to further prove it to ourselves.

Imagine being blindfolded right now. In such a state, can you still see? Your initial answer is probably "no," but think deeper about it. How can you *know* that you are blindfolded? If you cannot *see*, then how can you *know* that you cannot see? You can see the blindfold or the back of your eyelids, right? Therefore, you can *see* darkness. There is a subtle but major difference between not being able to see versus being able to see darkness. Which statement is more accurate to your experiences? The blindfold inhibits light from entering your eyes, but does it actually inhibit your *ability* to see? Does it affect your *awareness* at all? If it does, then how would you even *know* or *be aware* that you are blindfolded? How would you *know* the difference between light and darkness?

Think back to your earliest memories as a child. When you looked at the sky back then, were you *aware* of the clouds? Now, years later, when you step outside and look toward the sky, what has changed? Well, obviously the clouds look different. You are in a different place with a different set of conditions that brings about the unique scene before your eyes. But that part of you that *knew* you saw clouds when you were a kid – did that "knowing" ability of yours change after all these years? You can say that your eyes have gotten worse due to age, or perhaps your memory is no longer as sharp as it once was; but all these descriptions still depend on an *awareness* of your change! Did this *awareness* deteriorate with your body? Did your ability to *know* – not how well you perceive through your senses, but simply your ability to *know* – get any older since you were a child? Did it lose its inherent clarity? Do these questions even make sense, given the fact that your *perception* and *awareness* cannot be conveyed with words?

This brings us to an ancient, philosophical riddle that challenges our rational minds: Can a blind man see? If he were born blind, how can he still "see?" Even though he may not "see" the world in the same way we do, he still *knows*. He still has the *ability* to *know*. He is still *aware* of his thoughts. While awareness is intimately tied to our senses, it fundamentally rests underneath them. If our physical sense organs fail, our *awareness* does not. So, without requiring a major leap of faith, we can begin to see that part of us that "continues" after death. "Continues" is placed within quotes here because continuity is but an illusion of time. If our *awareness* does not change, how can it come into being or cease to be? How can it "travel" anywhere? It is simply *ever present*. How can it ever die? What do we have to fear? This sheds another ray of light on the practice of living in the present moment. If that part of us that matters most seems to transcend the illusion of time, is there anything beyond the present? This enters a deeper philosophical territory that is beyond the scope of this discussion, but perhaps this can inspire further reflection. Clearly, the meanings and practical applications of the symbolic evergreen sprig of the Master Mason degree are boundless.

Through our critical analyses of the *unconditioned* nature of our pure and spotless *awareness*, we see an endless list of applications to our daily lives. Each realization we obtain along this journey takes us one step closer to a more fulfilling and meaningful life. With no end in sight, we continue to walk, improving our world and ourselves each and every step of the way. By understanding our *current* experiences, we live life more fully. By abiding in our evergreen sprig of inner awareness, ever seeking the inherent wisdom of our true nature, we approach the ultimate secret of a Master Mason – a reward that we can only discover for ourselves.

While continuing our journey, we must ever search for the lost word and the evergreen sprig. We are like actors who perform in a play. When the time comes and the curtains of our physical bodies fall, our stage roles terminate. At that point, we merely remove our costumes and continue forward. Unlike the characters, who change from play to play, we are the actors, who remain unchanged between plays. What continues onward after the end of a play is the true nature of the character. What lies beneath the awesome waves of the sea is a boundless ocean. What allows the existence of beautiful snowflakes is the great atmosphere. What enables our life experiences is the mind. All that is temporary rests on the unconditioned.

Let us continue to train ourselves to more fully understand the subtle beauty and magnificence of the empty canvas, the ocean, the air, and the mind – symbols for all the things that allow the ephemeral to exist, but are all too often neglected. Only then can we appreciate that which transcends the dualities of the temporal. Only then can we rest at ease, knowing that true happiness and contentment is merely within our grasp of that evergreen sprig, no matter the circumstance. Let us go forth and continue searching for the lost traveler.

VII

Toward the Light

OUR TEACHERS

We have come a long way, my brother. The journey we've walked has been difficult, oftentimes grueling, and completely unpredictable. Certain sections of the trail were steep and dark, but as you know, what may have seemed difficult at the time may often become the most valuable moments in our lives. Reflecting on earlier years in my life, I can remember those tortuous moments that ultimately led to bigger and brighter opportunities. In hindsight, those moments really weren't that bad. On the other hand, there have been circumstances that seemed wonderful at the time but did not evolve in the way I had hoped. We all share the same predicament. So what should we make of this? How can we deal with the unpredictability of life?

Preparation is the best antidote to uncertainty. When we treat problems before they grow into catastrophes, we reduce their negative impacts later down the trail. But we must be wary not to rush to conclusions and act impulsively under the guise of preparation, only to be trapped in our limited perspectives. This balance is how we should continue navigating our river of life. In addition, we must be ever mindful of the symbol of the beehive. Like a swarm of bees, all of humanity must work together or the individuals who isolate themselves will fall behind. We depend on each other, and we rely on the fruits of each other's labors. Regardless of the unpredictability of life, we know that our hard work will always pay off; it is only a matter of when. Sooner or later, under the right causes and conditions, a tree will most certainly bear fruit. So let us continue with the fixed and steady resolve to do what is best for humanity and the world.

But how do we determine when something is a problem? Since only a fine line may separate a blessing and a curse, how are we to know when something is good or bad? Here, the wise Master Mason will immediately invoke the symbol of the checkered pavement and realize that these questions are merely an illusion brought about by our limited perspectives. There is an ancient folktale that can help illustrate this reality.

Once upon a time, in a rural area of the country, a farmer lived with his family. They owned a plot of land and worked long hours. They were known for their diligence. But one morning, one of the farmer's horses escaped into the hills. A neighbor came by in sadness to express his sympathy for the farmer's bad luck. "Bad luck? Good luck? Who knows?" was the farmer's reply. Days later, the horse returned, bringing back several other horses from the hills. Upon seeing this, the neighbor exclaimed in joy and congratulated the farmer on his good luck. "Good luck? Bad luck? Who knows?" the farmer said calmly. One day, the farmer's son, in an attempt to tame one of the horses, fell off the saddle and broke his leg. The neighbor returned to offer his condolences and wondered about the farmer's bad luck. "Bad luck? Good luck? Who knows?" was the farmer's only response. A few weeks later, the kingdom entered a war and was short on troops. The military mandated conscription and came through the countryside to collect all able-bodied young men to fight on the front lines. Upon seeing the son's broken leg, they passed over him. The neighbor was so thankful that the life of the farmer's son would not be at risk and lauded the farmer's good luck. Again, the farmer remained calm and simply responded, "Good luck? Bad luck? Who knows?"

Since life does not deal with absolutes, why fret over the individual events in our lives that we cannot control? We should accept things as they come and do our best to prepare for the future. Once we have done our best, we should let go of our worries. When things go extremely well for us, when the "laurel leaves of victory" rest on our shoulders, we should remember the less fortunate and remain humble. When things do not go as planned, when struggles seem to smother our ability to continue, we must brush the sweat from our faces and remain hopeful. All things are relative, including the events in our lives.

To overcome adversity, we must accept its challenge. We should see all the negative events and people in our lives as nothing but challenges that train us to become better people. By testing our patience and inner strength, they may actually be doing us a tremendous service in the long run. In this manner, those who stand in our way are not our enemies, but rather, our teachers. Sometimes, the best teachers in hindsight are the most difficult ones to endure in foresight. The good events and people in our lives are also our teachers, for they encourage us to continue our journey with our heads held high. Both the good and the bad form the quilt – the checkered pavement – of our lives. To mentally transcend duality is to see both sides as crucial components of our journey.

How we view and deal with each individual situation is our choice. Why not treat all things as ways to improve ourselves? This mindset gives us the strength and the fortitude to continue in the face of the most trying times. It boosts our inner strength to endure the most challenging of situations. Many in the past who have survived the most terrible atrocities in human history have embodied this spirit of fortitude. Viktor Frankl, a survivor of the Auschwitz concentration camp during the

Holocaust, wrote these inspirational words in his famous book, *Man's Search for Meaning*:

We who lived in concentration camps can remember the men who walked through the huts comforting others, giving away their last piece of bread. They may have been few in number, but they offer sufficient proof that everything can be taken from a man but one thing: the last of the human freedoms – to choose one's attitude in any given set of circumstances, to choose one's own way.

This mentality, that the human mind *always* has the ability to choose its attitude toward any situation, for better or for worse, embodies the greatest lesson that any Master Mason can learn. Frankl's words serve as a testament to the value of letting go of our extreme emotions and passions. When we succeed in that fundamental task of a Mason, we see the value of freeing our minds from the "vices and superfluities of life." Rather than being a slave to our passions, we become a master of ourselves. We manifest the inherent ability of our minds to cut our own paths – to carry us through our journey of life. We build that "house not made with hands." We become a true Master Mason.

During the brutal apartheid era of South Africa, would-be President Nelson Mandela survived 27 years in prison, suffering under brutal conditions. His perseverance and eventual release upon the end of decades of racial segregation in South Africa hinged on a poem written by British poet William Ernest Henley in 1875. Mandela recited this poem, entitled "Invictus," to himself and fellow prisoners while confined on Robben Island, which ultimately gave him the strength and fortitude to conquer the odds:

Out of the night that covers me,
Black as the pit from pole to pole,

I thank whatever gods may be
For my unconquerable soul.

In the fell clutch of circumstance
I have not winced nor cried aloud.
Under the bludgeonings of chance
My head is bloody, but unbowed.

Beyond this place of wrath and tears
Looms but the Horror of the shade,
And yet the menace of the years
Finds, and shall find me, unafraid.

It matters not how strait the gate,
How charged with punishments the scroll.
I am the master of my fate:
I am the captain of my soul.

My brother, no matter how difficult the times, how impossible the odds, or how painful the circumstance, keep the faith and never give up. In the words of Brother Douglas MacArthur:

Years wrinkle the skin, but to give up enthusiasm wrinkles the soul.

Each blow to your ego, each challenge to your life, and each test of your fidelity is but one of your greatest and most demanding teachers. Look around. Even the most benign of objects and phenomena in nature have been your teachers on this journey. We are surrounded by animate and inanimate objects that all have something to teach us. We just need to notice them. Think back along our journey. Aside from Masonic symbols, the world at large has given us great insight. A cave taught us about ignorance, a car taught us about change, an optical illusion taught us about dualities, a guitar string taught us about balance, a bicycle taught us about living in the present, a candle taught us about kindness, a train taught us about emotions, and the water taught us about the nature of life. Look around. The divine is written in the scripture that is the natural world. It surrounds us. There is a wealth of wisdom to be learned both inside and outside the lodge room. All we have to do is *pay attention.*

THE POT OF GOLD

It is not the amount of time a man has been a Mason that matters; what matters most is the amount of *attention* he gives the symbols and the degree of *practice* he devotes to applying those philosophies to his daily life. Titles and fame do not determine the Mason. He who has truly mastered the lost word and finished the unfinished work in *his* sanctum sanctorum would not care for titles and names, for they cannot even come close to that glorious and magnificent feeling of joy and accomplishment that comes from the realization of true wisdom and a life well lived. As Brother George Washington said:

I hope I shall possess firmness and virtue enough to maintain what I consider the most enviable of all titles, the character of an honest man.

As responsible Master Masons, lest our forefathers' work was done in vain, it is our *duty* to educate and encourage the youngest members of our fraternity to seek the light of wisdom and build a better world. There are no shortcuts. We all must walk the journey and *experience* it for ourselves. But Masonic philosophy should not and cannot be force-fed. Each person must be inspired from within himself to care.

By encouraging the new initiate to reach upward in the pursuit of *Truth*, he will naturally see for himself that he truly stands on the level with his fellow brothers. This would then inspire his contribution to *Brotherly Love* and to the *Relief* of those who are less fortunate, within and outside the fraternity.

You and I left the trailhead and started this journey together, with a mutual interest to improve ourselves and help each other do so. I am happy to say, my brother, that it was time well spent. Let us now go on to inspire others on this journey. While we are still not perfect, nor is the institution of Freemasonry, we are crucial links that lead to the distant goals of Truth and virtue. While we may not have yet stepped completely into the light outside the cave, we are well on our way. We see it off in the distance. But there is still much work to do — work that must be done through *inspiration*, more so than merely education. In the words of Brother Antoine de Saint-Exupery:

If you want to build a ship, don't heard people together to collect wood and don't assign them tasks and work, but rather teach them to long for the endless immensity of the sea.

A person who leads by example does not need to win respect, for he naturally commands it through his actions framed in humility, understanding, and compassion. And so, let us make the most out of each waking moment, to improve ourselves while helping others do the same. Only then can our work become that noblest of charities that extends beyond the grave.

Remember that pot of gold I promised you when we began our journey? In the words of an unknown author:

> *You came with me on a long arduous journey,*
> *Through many forests and jungles;*
> *The paths confusing and twisted,*
> *Sometimes, I made you miss a turning;*
> *There was no promised pot of gold.*
> *But then my brethren, it is not the gold;*
> *It was the search itself;*
> *The journey and your comradeship,*
> *The jungles we saw*
> *The forests we conquered*
> *The rivers we forded,*
> *And the links we made.*
> *It would not have happened*
> *If it was not for the pot of gold.*

The light that we seek is not a destination, but an ongoing process. The journey itself *is* the pot of gold. At the end of this expedition, we find peace of mind – the contentment and fulfillment that comes with successfully seeing past our own habits, biases, and egos. The ideas inculcated by Masonry then come naturally to us with little effort. The joy and happiness that results from this peace of mind is something that nobody can take away, because it is grounded on personal *experience* and *practice*.

When is a man a Mason? There has been no better answer to this question than the one posed in 1914 by Brother Joseph Fort Newton in his book, *The Builders*:

When he can look out over the rivers, the hills, and the far horizon with a profound sense of his own littleness in the vast scheme of things, and yet have faith, hope, and courage – which is the root of every virtue.

When he knows that down in his heart every man is as noble, as vile, as divine, as diabolic, and as lonely as himself, and seeks to know, to forgive, and to love his fellow man.

When he knows how to sympathize with men in their sorrows, yea, even in their sins — knowing that each man fights a hard fight against many odds.

When he has learned how to make friends and to keep them, and above all how to keep friends with himself.

When he loves flowers, can hunt birds without a gun, and feels the thrill of an old forgotten joy when he hears the laugh of a little child.

When he can be happy and high-minded amid the meaner drudgeries of life.

When star-crowned trees, and the glint of sunlight on flowing waters, subdue him like the thought of one much loved and long dead.

When no voice of distress reaches his ears in vain, and no hand seeks his aid without response.

When he finds good in every faith that helps any man to lay hold of divine things and sees majestic meanings in life, whatever the name of that faith may be.

When he can look into a wayside puddle and see something beyond mud, and into the face of the most forlorn fellow mortal and see something beyond sin.

When he knows how to pray, how to love, how to hope.

When he has kept faith with himself, with his fellow man, and with his God; in his hand a sword for evil, in his heart a bit of a song — glad to live, but not afraid to die!

Such a man has found the only real secret of Masonry, and the one which it is trying to give to all the world.

Alas, our time together is quickly drawing to a close. I am happy that we had the chance to walk a brief segment of this journey together. It has been a true pleasure, but it is time for our rivers of life to diverge. Perhaps we will cross paths again someday. For now, as we walk across the sand dunes of time, never forget that each footprint we leave behind tells a story. Let each story be a testament to your honor, integrity, and compassion. It is up to you to determine the contents of the following pages. Till we meet again, I bid you fair winds and safe travels. Strive on, my brother. Strive on!

Truth will ultimately prevail
where there are pains to bring it to light.

~ Brother George Washington

Reflections

This last section is for you to record your personal thoughts. Use the concepts and ideas in this book as a launching point for your own realizations as you continue your journey. Someday, perhaps you will find that what you wrote here changed your life for the better. May these pages serve as your trusty companion as you continue walking your trail of life. Best wishes to your adventure!

Date: _____ Chapter: _____ Page: _____
Thoughts:

_____

_____

_____

_____

_____

_____

_____

_____

_____

_____

_____

_____

_____

_____

_____

_____

_____

Date: _____ Chapter: _____ Page: _____
Thoughts:
_____
_____
_____
_____
_____
_____
_____
_____
_____
_____
_____
_____

Date: _____ Chapter: _____ Page: _____
Thoughts:
_____
_____
_____
_____
_____
_____
_____
_____
_____
_____
_____
_____

Date: _____ Chapter: _____ Page: _____
Thoughts:

_____
_____
_____
_____
_____
_____
_____
_____
_____
_____
_____

Date: _____ Chapter: _____ Page: _____
Thoughts:

_____
_____
_____
_____
_____
_____
_____
_____
_____
_____
_____

Date: _____ Chapter: _____ Page: _____
Thoughts:

_____
_____
_____
_____
_____
_____
_____
_____
_____
_____
_____

Date: _____ Chapter: _____ Page: _____
Thoughts:

_____
_____
_____
_____
_____
_____
_____
_____
_____
_____
_____

Date: _____ Chapter: _____ Page: _____
Thoughts:

_____
_____
_____
_____
_____
_____
_____
_____
_____
_____
_____
_____

Date: _____ Chapter: _____ Page: _____
Thoughts:

_____
_____
_____
_____
_____
_____
_____
_____
_____
_____
_____
_____

Date: _____ Chapter: _____ Page: _____
Thoughts:
_____
_____
_____
_____
_____
_____
_____
_____
_____
_____
_____

Date: _____ Chapter: _____ Page: _____
Thoughts:
_____
_____
_____
_____
_____
_____
_____
_____
_____
_____
_____

Date: _____ Chapter: _____ Page: _____
Thoughts:
_____
_____
_____
_____
_____
_____
_____
_____
_____
_____
_____

Date: _____ Chapter: _____ Page: _____
Thoughts:
_____
_____
_____
_____
_____
_____
_____
_____
_____
_____

Date: _____ Chapter: _____ Page: _____
Thoughts:
_____
_____
_____
_____
_____
_____
_____
_____
_____
_____

Date: _____ Chapter: _____ Page: _____
Thoughts:
_____
_____
_____
_____
_____
_____
_____
_____
_____
_____

Date: _____ Chapter: _____ Page: _____
Thoughts:

_____
_____
_____
_____
_____
_____
_____
_____
_____
_____
_____
_____

Date: _____ Chapter: _____ Page: _____
Thoughts:

_____
_____
_____
_____
_____
_____
_____
_____
_____
_____
_____

Date: _____ Chapter: _____ Page: _____
Thoughts:

_____
_____
_____
_____
_____
_____
_____
_____
_____
_____
_____

Date: _____ Chapter: _____ Page: _____
Thoughts:

_____
_____
_____
_____
_____
_____
_____
_____
_____
_____
_____

Date: _____ Chapter: _____ Page: _____
Thoughts:

_____
_____
_____
_____
_____
_____
_____
_____
_____
_____
_____
_____

Date: _____ Chapter: _____ Page: _____
Thoughts:

_____
_____
_____
_____
_____
_____
_____
_____
_____
_____
_____

Date: _____ Chapter: _____ Page: _____
Thoughts:

_____

_____

_____

_____

_____

_____

_____

_____

_____

_____

Date: _____ Chapter: _____ Page: _____
Thoughts:

_____

_____

_____

_____

_____

_____

_____

_____

_____

_____

Date: _____ Chapter: _____ Page: _____
Thoughts:
_____
_____
_____
_____
_____
_____
_____
_____
_____
_____
_____
_____

Date: _____ Chapter: _____ Page: _____
Thoughts:
_____
_____
_____
_____
_____
_____
_____
_____
_____
_____
_____

Date: _____ Chapter: _____ Page: _____
Thoughts:
_____
_____
_____
_____
_____
_____
_____
_____
_____
_____
_____

Date: _____ Chapter: _____ Page: _____
Thoughts:
_____
_____
_____
_____
_____
_____
_____
_____
_____
_____
_____

Date: _____ Chapter: _____ Page: _____
Thoughts:

_____
_____
_____
_____
_____
_____
_____
_____
_____
_____
_____
_____

Date: _____ Chapter: _____ Page: _____
Thoughts:

_____
_____
_____
_____
_____
_____
_____
_____
_____
_____
_____

Date: _____ Chapter: _____ Page: _____
Thoughts:

_____
_____
_____
_____
_____
_____
_____
_____
_____
_____

Date: _____ Chapter: _____ Page: _____
Thoughts:

_____
_____
_____
_____
_____
_____
_____
_____
_____
_____

Date: _____ Chapter: _____ Page: _____
Thoughts:

_____

_____

_____

_____

_____

_____

_____

_____

_____

_____

_____

Date: _____ Chapter: _____ Page: _____
Thoughts:

_____

_____

_____

_____

_____

_____

_____

_____

_____

_____

_____

Date: _____ Chapter: _____ Page: _____
Thoughts:
_____
_____
_____
_____
_____
_____
_____
_____
_____
_____
_____

Date: _____ Chapter: _____ Page: _____
Thoughts:
_____
_____
_____
_____
_____
_____
_____
_____
_____
_____
_____

Date: _____ Chapter: _____ Page: _____
Thoughts:

_____
_____
_____
_____
_____
_____
_____
_____
_____
_____
_____
_____

Date: _____ Chapter: _____ Page: _____
Thoughts:

_____
_____
_____
_____
_____
_____
_____
_____
_____
_____
_____
_____

Date: _____ Chapter: _____ Page: _____
Thoughts:

_____
_____
_____
_____
_____
_____
_____
_____
_____
_____

Date: _____ Chapter: _____ Page: _____
Thoughts:

_____
_____
_____
_____
_____
_____
_____
_____
_____
_____

Date: _____ Chapter: _____ Page: _____
Thoughts:

_____
_____
_____
_____
_____
_____
_____
_____
_____
_____
_____
_____

Date: _____ Chapter: _____ Page: _____
Thoughts:

_____
_____
_____
_____
_____
_____
_____
_____
_____
_____
_____

Date: _____ Chapter: _____ Page: _____
Thoughts:

_____
_____
_____
_____
_____
_____
_____
_____
_____
_____
_____

Date: _____ Chapter: _____ Page: _____
Thoughts:

_____
_____
_____
_____
_____
_____
_____
_____
_____
_____
_____

Date: _____ Chapter: _____ Page: _____
Thoughts:

_____
_____
_____
_____
_____
_____
_____
_____
_____
_____
_____

Date: _____ Chapter: _____ Page: _____
Thoughts:

_____
_____
_____
_____
_____
_____
_____
_____
_____
_____
_____

Date: _____ Chapter: _____ Page: _____
Thoughts:

_____

_____

_____

_____

_____

_____

_____

_____

_____

_____

Date: _____ Chapter: _____ Page: _____
Thoughts:

_____

_____

_____

_____

_____

_____

_____

_____

_____

_____

Date: _____ Chapter: _____ Page: _____
Thoughts:

_____
_____
_____
_____
_____
_____
_____
_____
_____
_____
_____

Date: _____ Chapter: _____ Page: _____
Thoughts:

_____
_____
_____
_____
_____
_____
_____
_____
_____
_____
_____

Date: _____ Chapter: _____ Page: _____
Thoughts:

_____
_____
_____
_____
_____
_____
_____
_____
_____
_____
_____

Date: _____ Chapter: _____ Page: _____
Thoughts:

_____
_____
_____
_____
_____
_____
_____
_____
_____
_____
_____

Made in the USA
Charleston, SC
31 January 2016